THE
APARTMENT
IN
BAB
EL-LOUK

Translated by
ELISABETH JAQUETTE

Published by Darf Publishers, 2017

Darf Publishers Ltd
277 West End Lane
West Hampstead
London
NW6 1QS

The Apartment in Bab el-Louk
Words: Donia Maher
Translation: Elisabeth Jaquette
Art: Ganzeer, p. 03-70
                Ahmad Nady, p. 71-79
Design: Ganzeer

Originally published as:

في شـقة بـاب اللـوق
دار ميريت — ٢٠١٣

Printed and bound by Alliance Print,
Bulgaria

First editon, 2017

ISBN-13: 978-1-85077-306-1

www.darfpublishers.co.uk

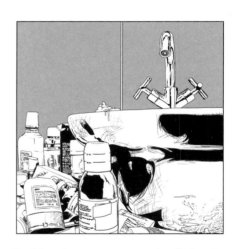

Inside the apartment in Bab el-Louk, my things are scattered everywhere, heaped up in piles around me, and there's no furniture to be seen. The water practically congeals in the tap, and soapsuds cling to the sides of the half-clogged bathroom sink. Containers of all shapes and sizes are stacked up high, filled with everything you can think of: make-up, creams, serums, hairspray, and deodorant (both scented and for sensitive skin).

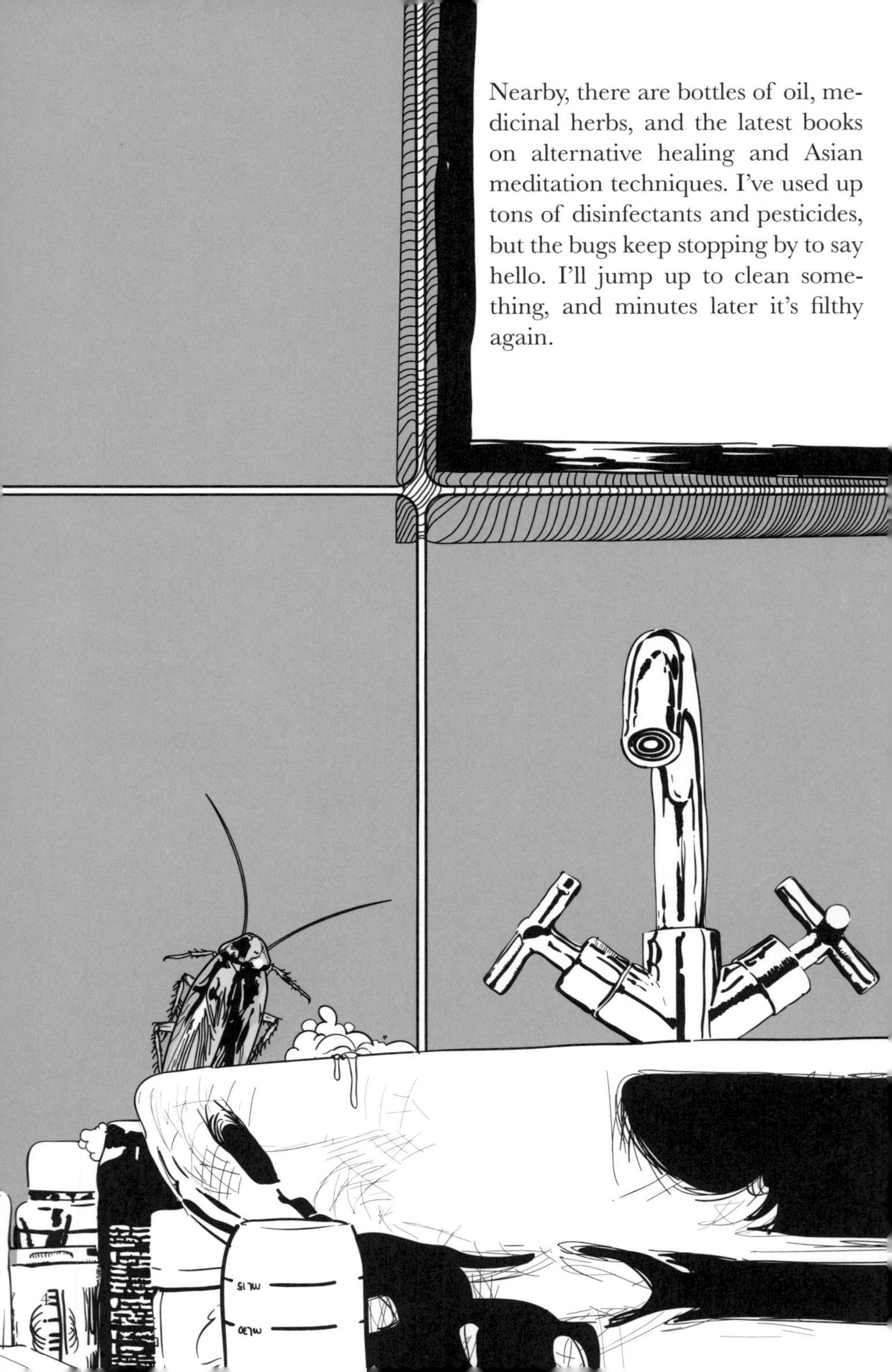
Nearby, there are bottles of oil, medicinal herbs, and the latest books on alternative healing and Asian meditation techniques. I've used up tons of disinfectants and pesticides, but the bugs keep stopping by to say hello. I'll jump up to clean something, and minutes later it's filthy again.
ml 15
ml 30

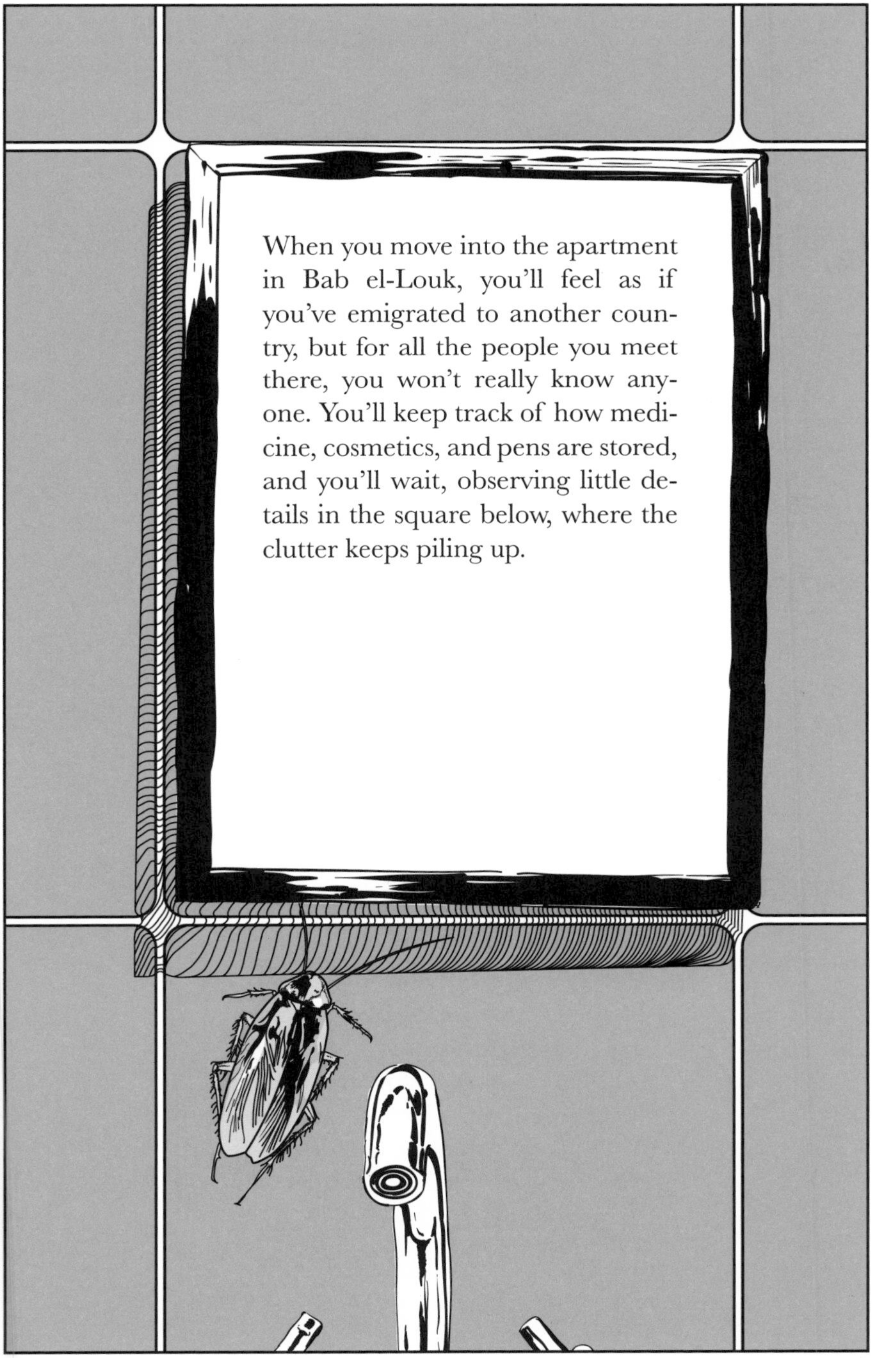
When you move into the apartment in Bab el-Louk, you'll feel as if you've emigrated to another country, but for all the people you meet there, you won't really know anyone. You'll keep track of how medicine, cosmetics, and pens are stored, and you'll wait, observing little details in the square below, where the clutter keeps piling up.

Outside your window, the crevices
of the city are lonely and forsaken,
like a deserted crime scene. Dis-
tant lights reveal themselves to you
furtively, never coming too close.
You'll keep your curtains drawn at
most hours, holding the sorrowful
square at bay.

Your suitcases will still be packed
and ready to go.

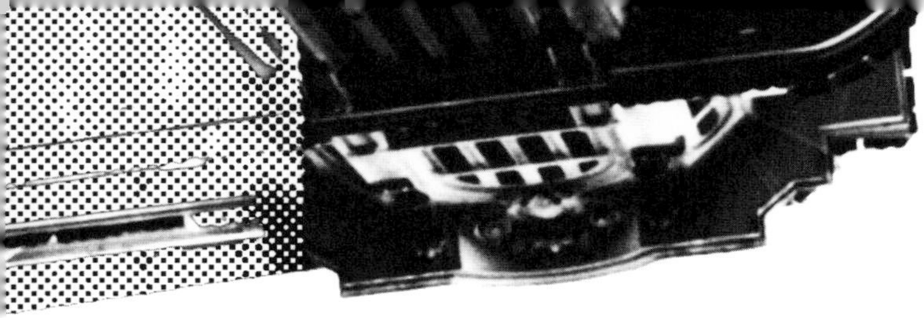

You'll feel like you're always being watched, like you're pressed for time – even in the doldrums of your day off, when you've got nothing to do.

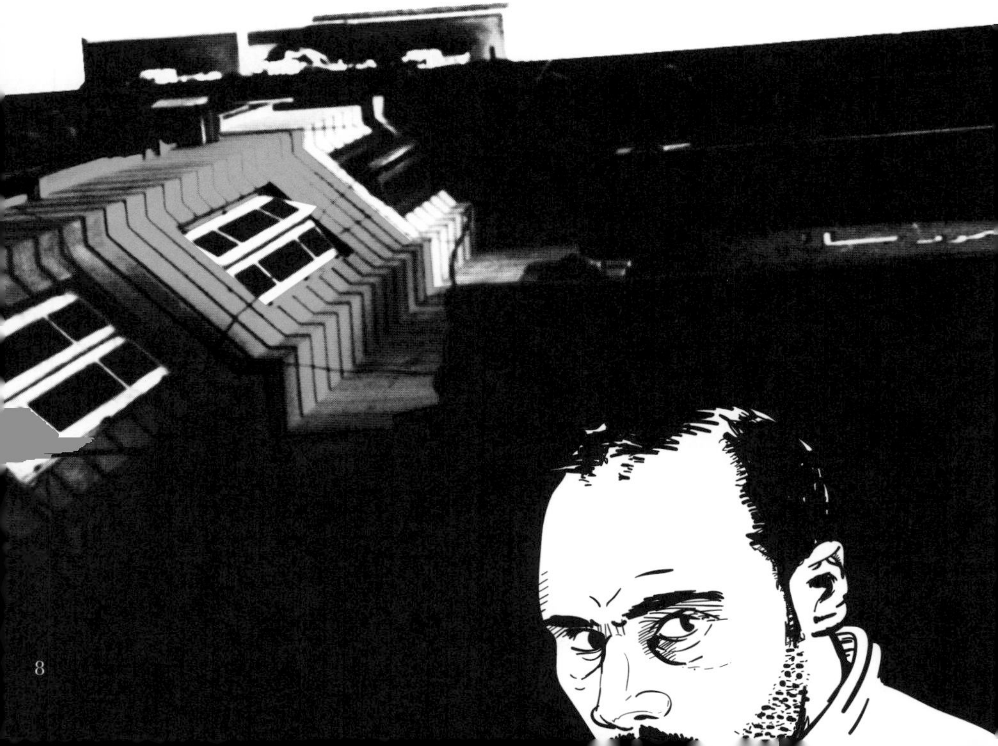

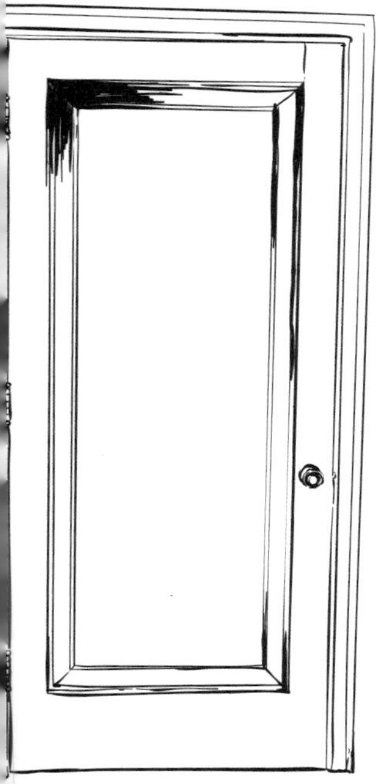

As a rule, you'll close the doors when you move from one room to the next, assiduously checking the windows.

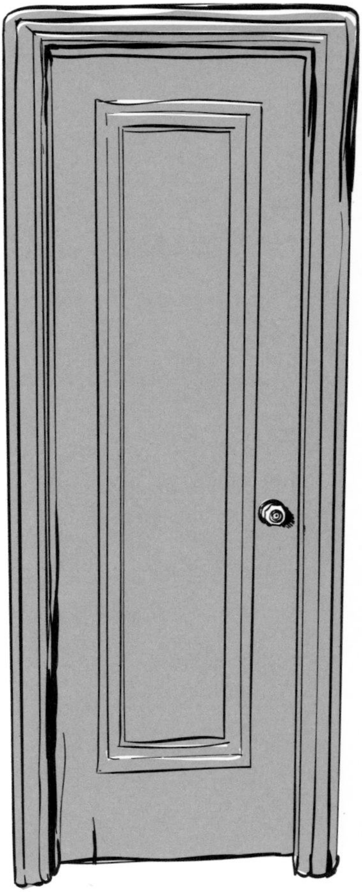

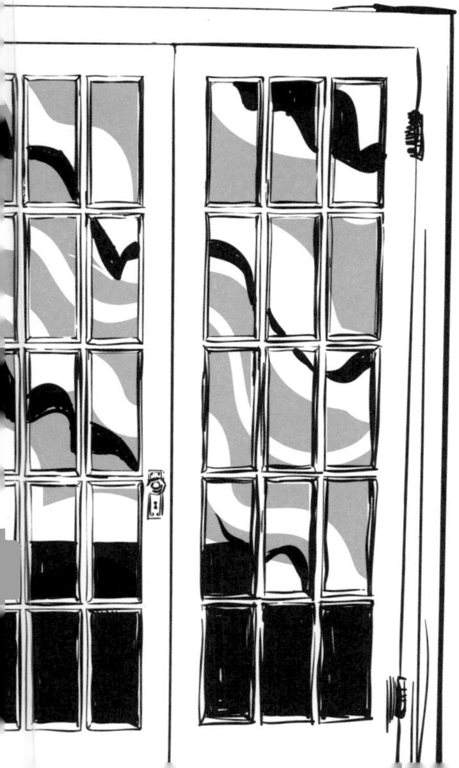

And there's that musty smell that never seems to leave.

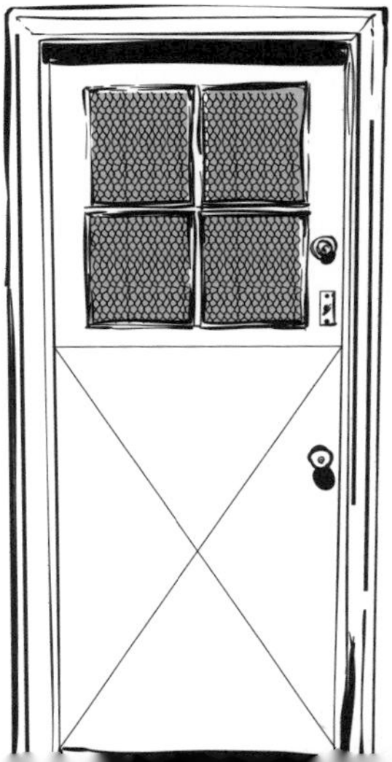

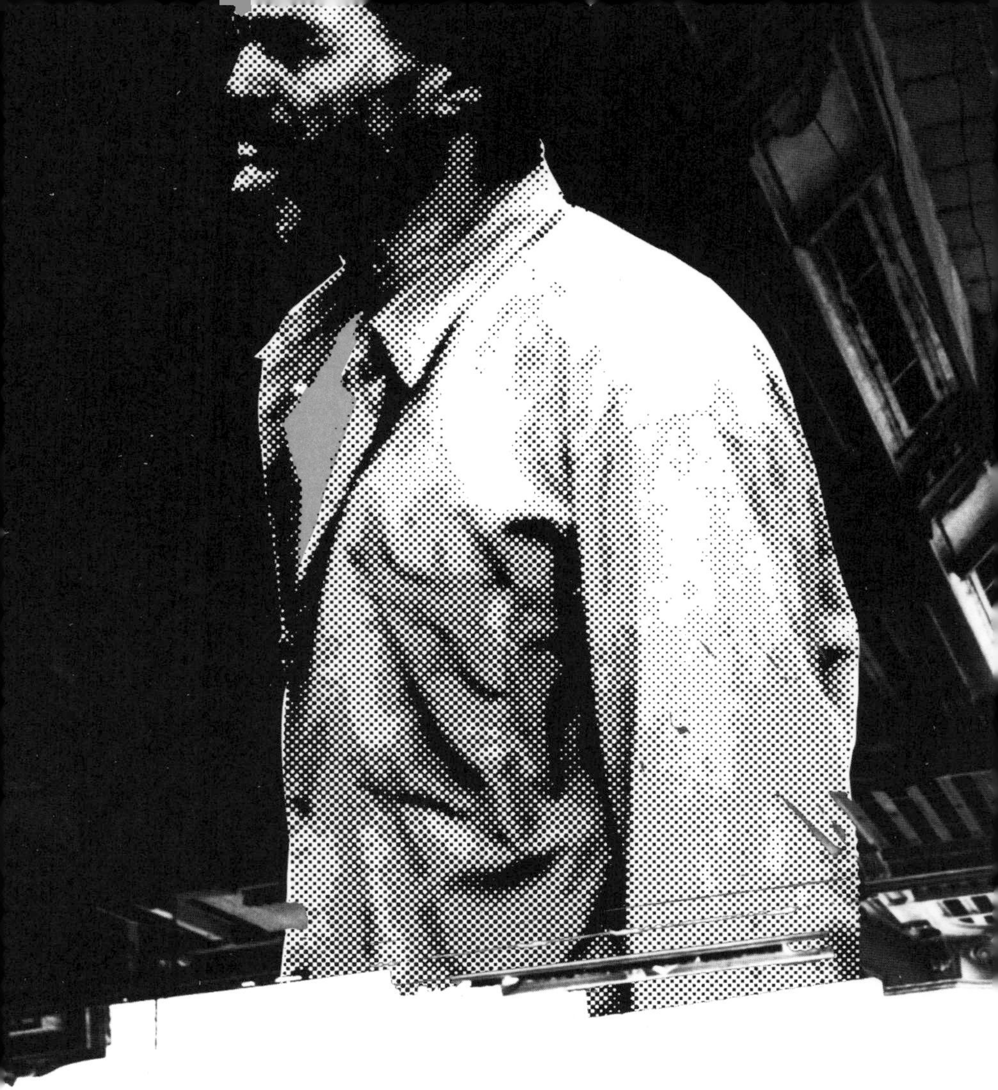

People passing through the square below inevitably notice you inside the apartment in Bab el-Louk, even though your head hardly peeks out from the tenth floor. You'll be scared, even though you've locked the door. You won't forget the way the mute man looks, standing on the street below your window, arguing with

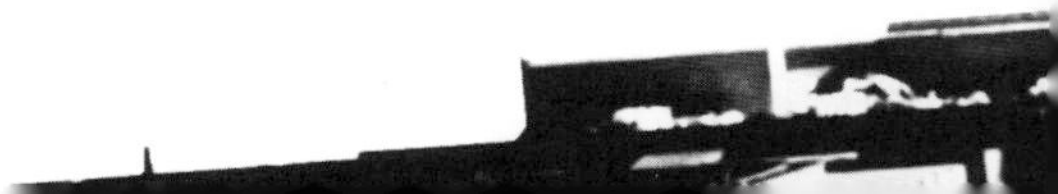

someone. Even without seeing him, you'll be able to tell where the other guy is, on the second floor balcony. The mute will scream, arms flailing above his head, suspended on tip-toe. Spooked, he'll take a couple of steps back. At first, he'll gesture for this mysterious character to descend from above and follow him.

Maybe it's a woman, you'll think. It looks like he's blowing her kisses, and he quickly mimes something suggestive, but the response appears to be rejection. Then the hand that channeled such affection will contort, sending vulgar notions coursing through its fingers. You won't understand the abrupt change. You'll look out cautiously, so he won't notice you and launch an insult-laden cry at you. Just because he's mute doesn't mean he can't express himself as plain as day.

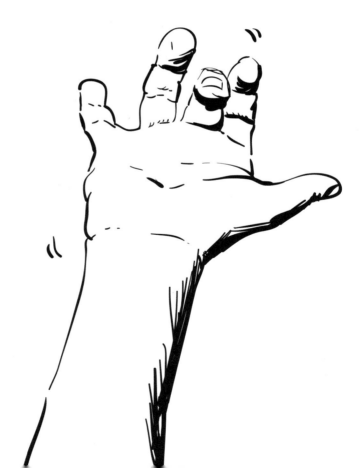

Suddenly, he'll spin around and cut across the square as if nothing happened, and when he fondly waves good-bye to the person standing on the balcony, bewilderment will trace its way along your eyebrows. Only now do you realize that the balcony the mute beggar was looking at actually belongs to an elderly doctor's clinic. You were there, once, and you remember that no one's allowed on the balcony. In fact, there is no balcony – just a plate-glass window with no handle, the whole thing sealed shut. Through the frosted glass, you could barely see the lights of the square. When you peer out from the apartment in Bab el-Louk, it's the crazies you'll be up against.

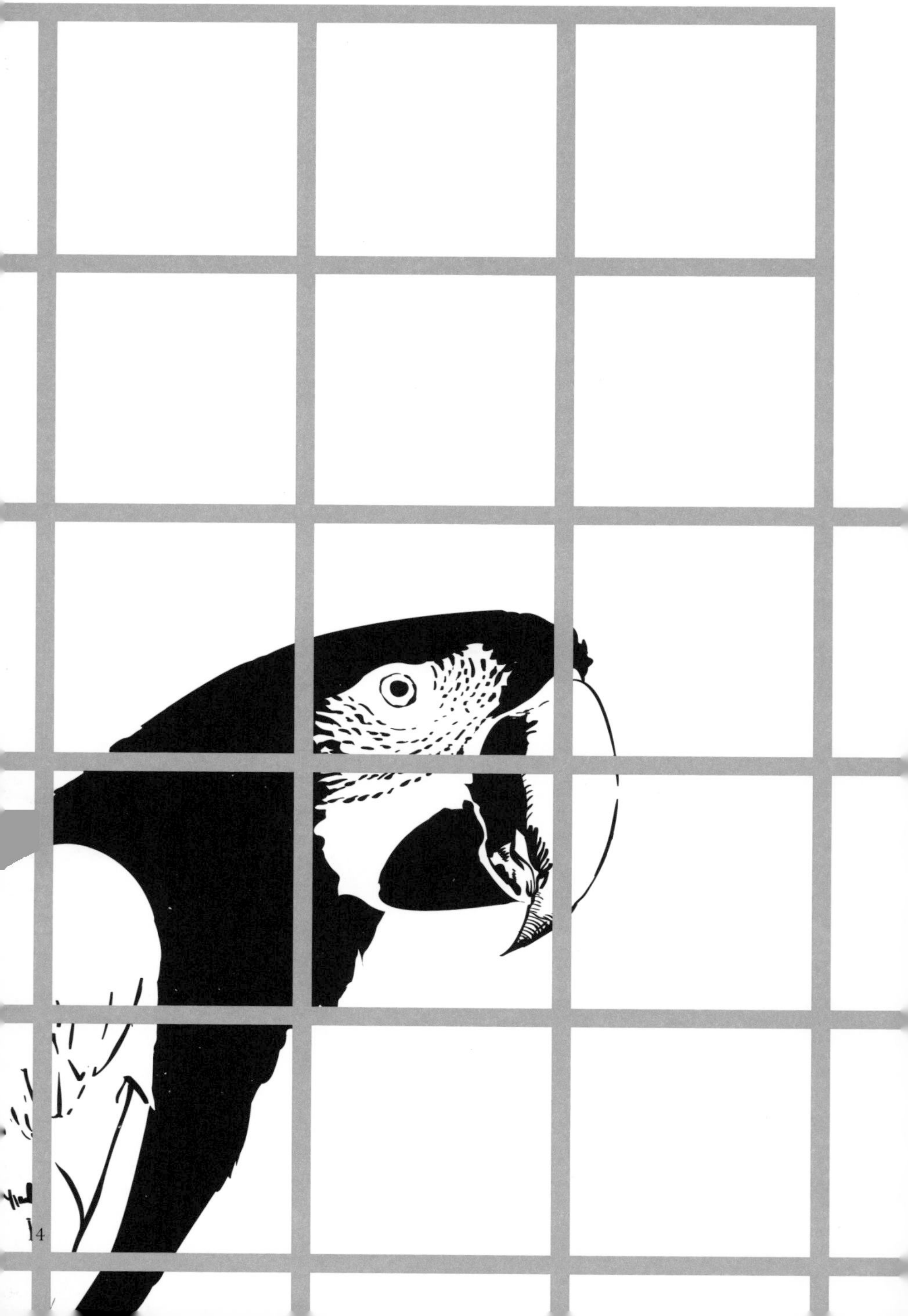

I grew used to a jesting voice, like the one that bursts forth from street vendors' lungs to draw attention to their wares. This voice called out my name at sunrise and sunset, so often that I began to look forward to it. When I was little, I always thought that the man who roamed the streets selling old dishware was calling out just to me. I won't be fooled so easily this time. I searched for the source of this voice that sounded so close, and to my surprise I realized it was a parrot. That is, a corner of a birdcage + mimicking the voices in the street = a parrot.

But why was it calling my name? I smiled.

At the time, I didn't know this game would repeat itself. When you come to rent the apartment in Bab el-Louk, the parrots will call you by name, and by nickname, and you'll become the laughingstock of the birds in the building across the way. Your only friend will bid you good evening, and every morning you'll make sure that there are enough sunflower seeds on the bottom of his cage. You'll ask yourself: should you bring him in from the balcony on biting winter nights? As the light changes, you'll wait for his voice to call to you, to reassure you that the ageing parrot still lives. You will believe that what exists between you is real; you will choose to ignore that everyone who lives where you do is enslaved to the birds.

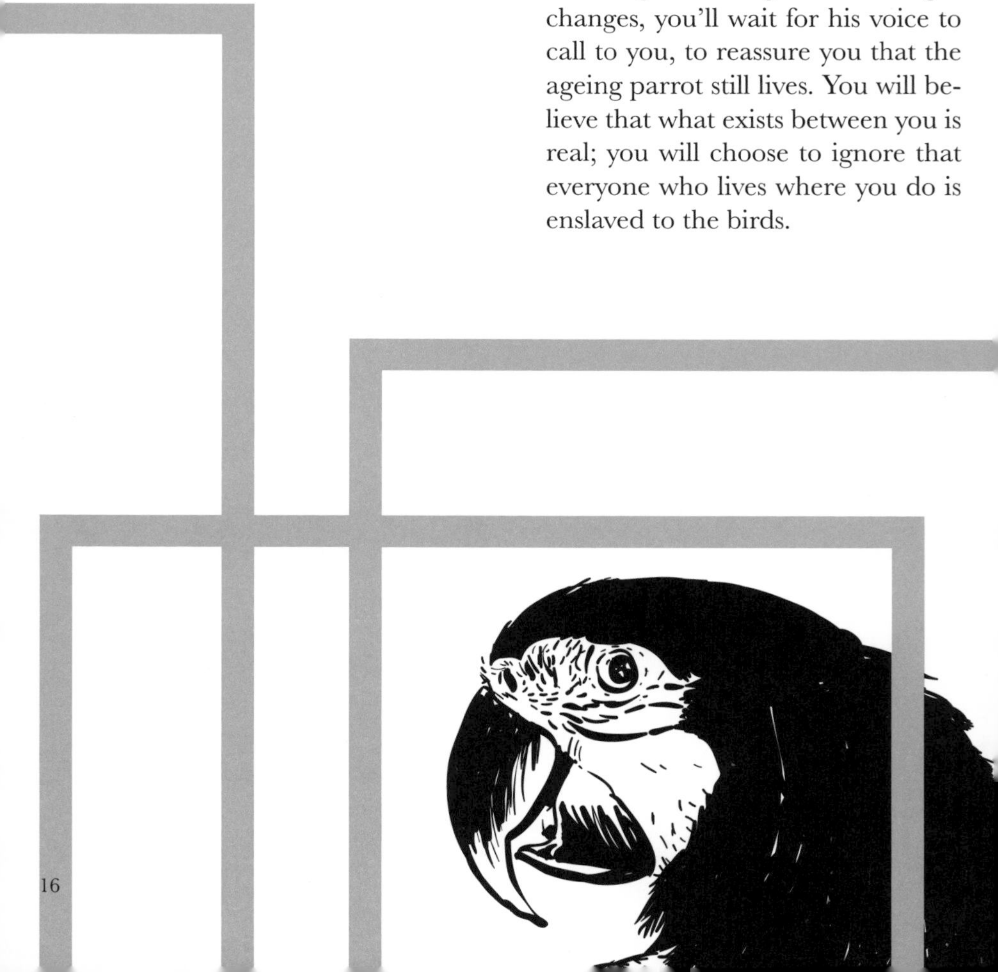

A cavalcade of cleaning ladies arrives at your apartment in Bab el-Louk. One after another they'll cheat you and steal things, until Um Ra'aey arrives, the one who will lull you to sleep with her sweet, soporific voice.

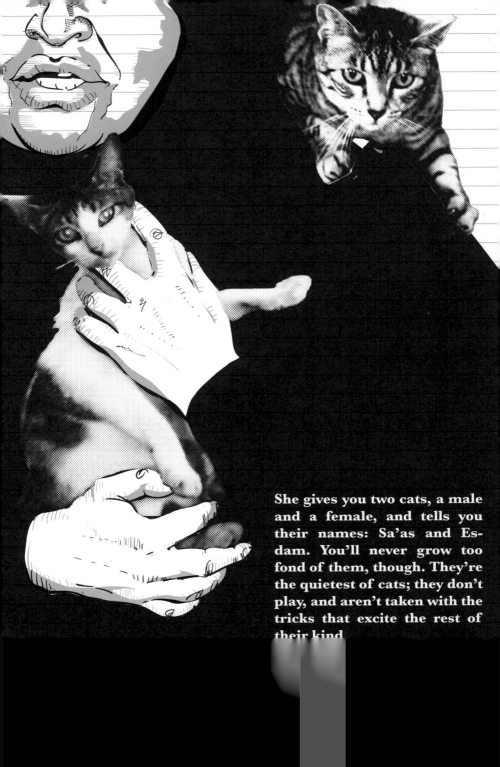

She gives you two cats, a male and a female, and tells you their names: Sa'as and Esdam. You'll never grow too fond of them, though. They're the quietest of cats; they don't play, and aren't taken with the tricks that excite the rest of their kind.

They
simply
follow
you
silently
from place
to place, occasionally ex-
changing words. You swear they'r
eavesdropping on
your phone calls, whispering
pern iciou sly;
they size up
your visi tors and

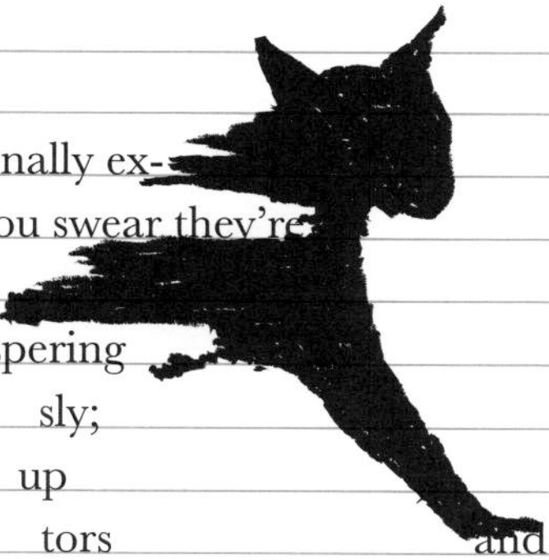

judge

your

every

move.

You'll try calling them: 'Psst, here kitty kitty! Here Mishmisha!' but they'll just ignore you or give you a withering stare.

Um Ra'aey will rollick through your apartment, and bring her two children to live with you. They'll speak as sleepily as she does, and you'll end up in the corner alone, next to a dish for food and water, under the happy family's care: Um Ra'aey, her son, his sister Bania, and their friends: Sa'as and Esdam.

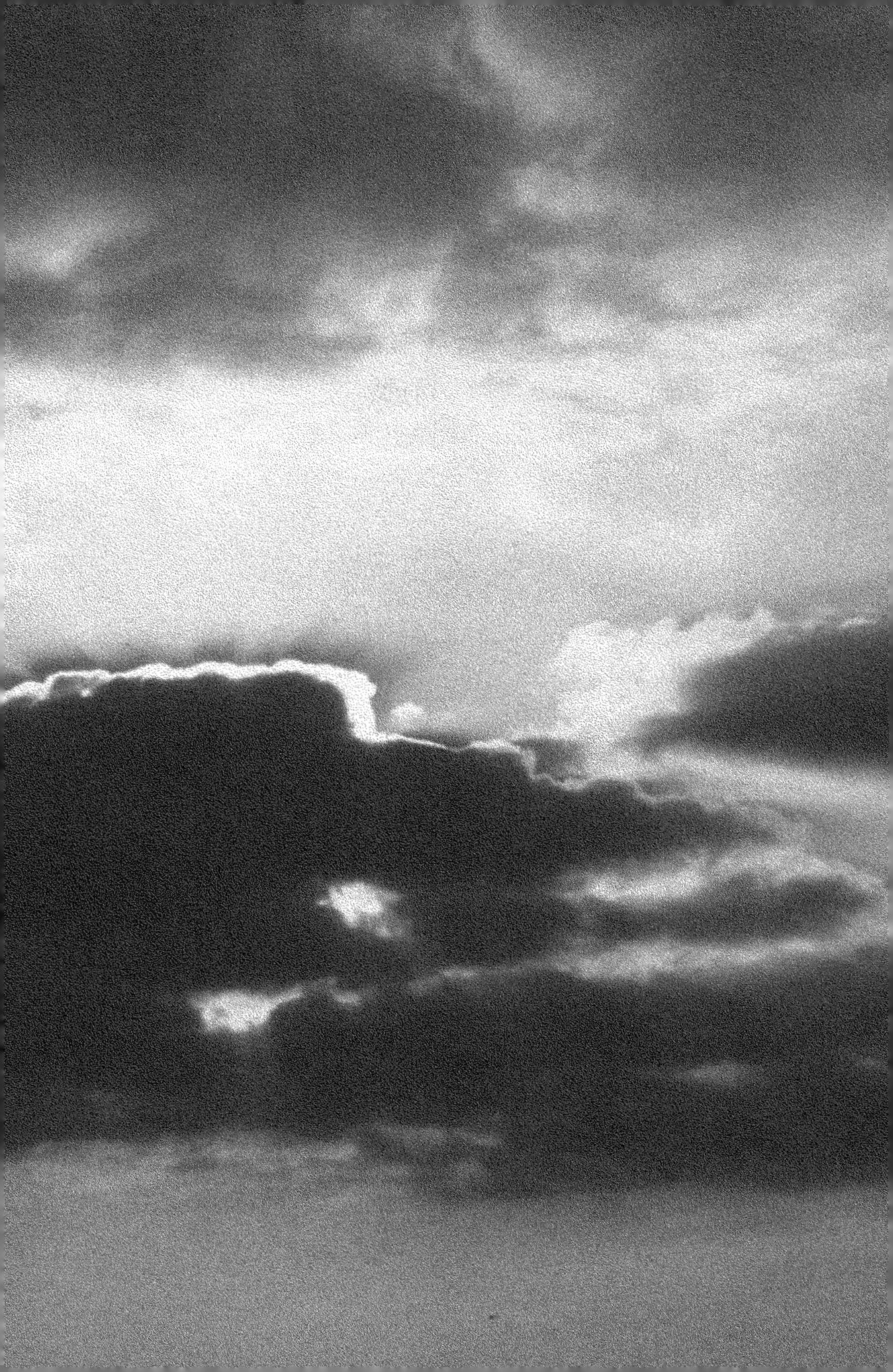

Sometimes,

you'll wake up in the apartment in Bab el-Louk to repeated cries:

ha ha ha ha ha ha

and you'll smile, amused, thinking someone out there's having fun.

He sounds so close,

ha ha ha

and whenever the rain falls, his voice lifts up.

ha ha ha

You'll be overcome by curiosity one day,

so you'll lean out the window to find out where it's coming from,

that breathless gleeful sigh,

ha ha ha

and then you'll see him.

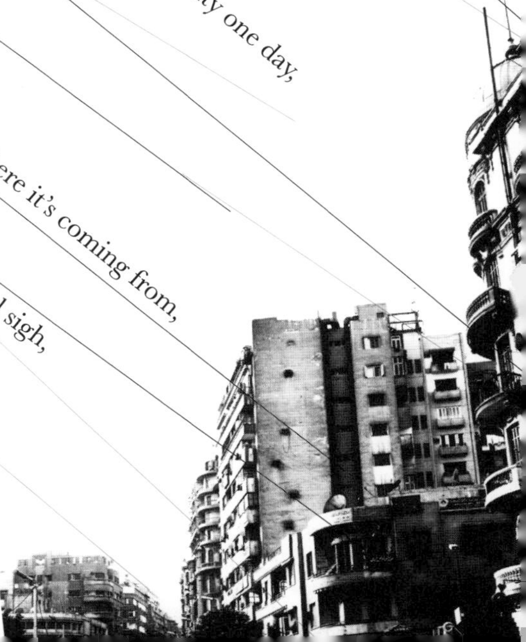

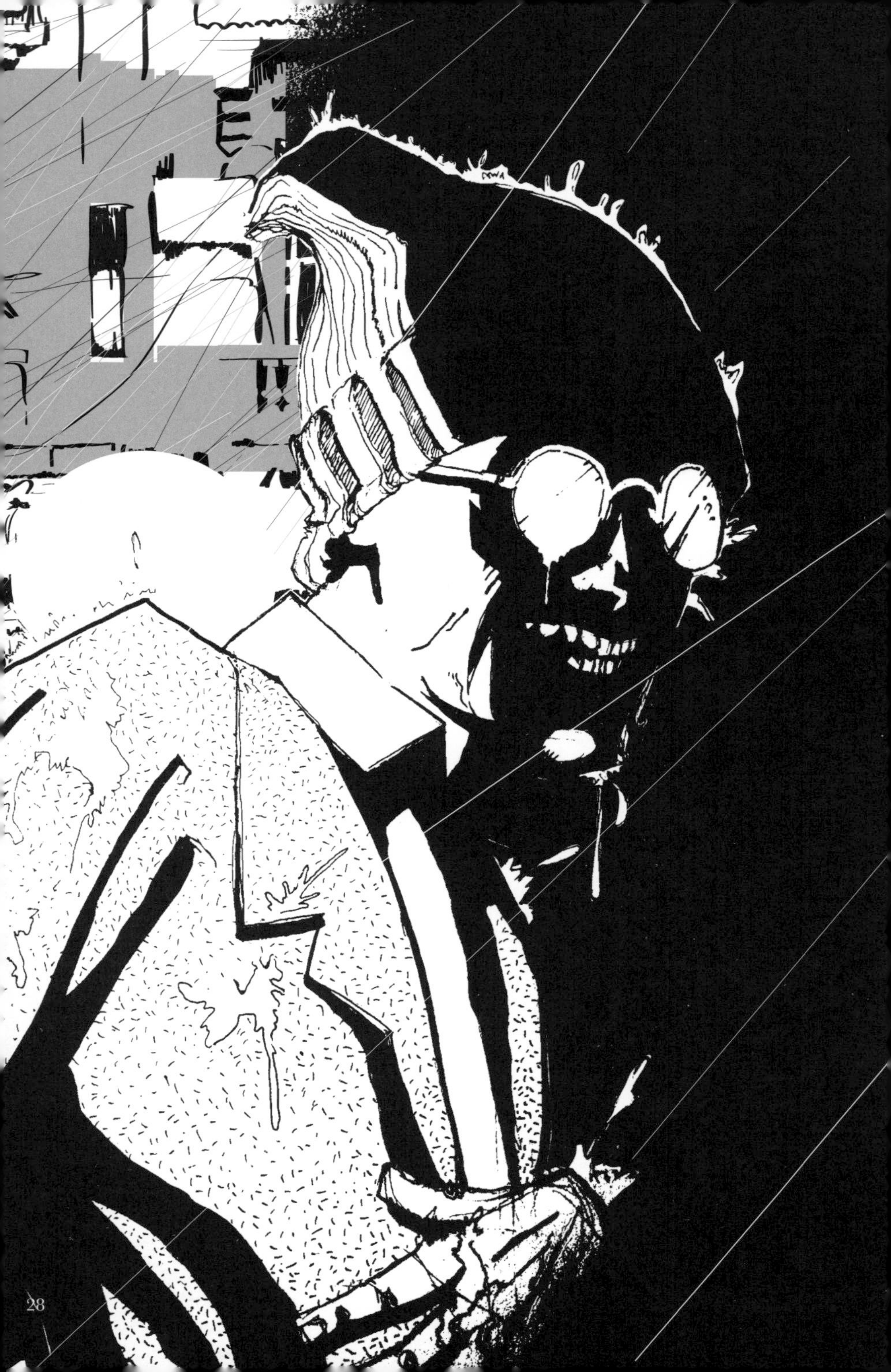

On the other side of the square, he skips around the sidewalk to a hastening *accelerando,* each leap launching him several meters in a different direction, his cries magnify, gradually, overtaking the first sounds of morning in the sodden square.

He lifts his face and shoulders to the heavens, where the muse for his joyful dance pours forth: the rain.

If it rains at night you won't be able to see him, but you'll still hear his laughter

ha ha ha

echoing in the buildings around the square. In the morning rain he dances next to el-Ayyat Farms shop, but when he emerges to dance for the night deluge, it's far from that usual spot.

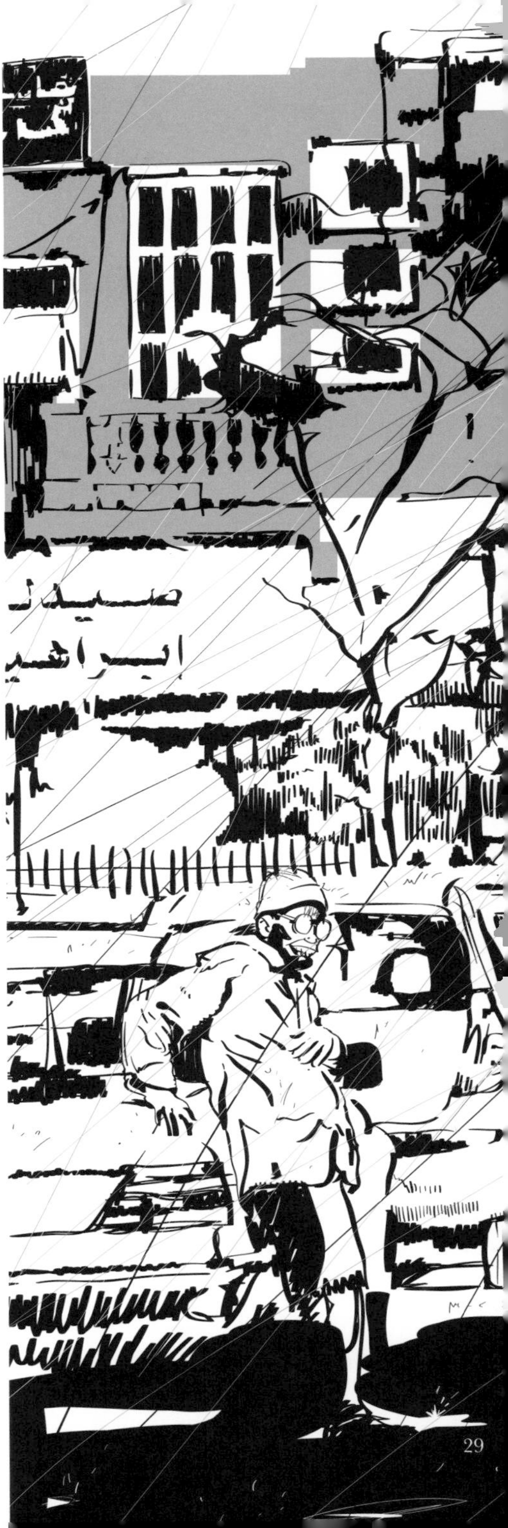

When you try to leave the apartment in Bab el-Louk, Hamada will stop you to tell you that he's hungry. He'll feebly point at his mouth, as if to say he doesn't have the strength to speak.

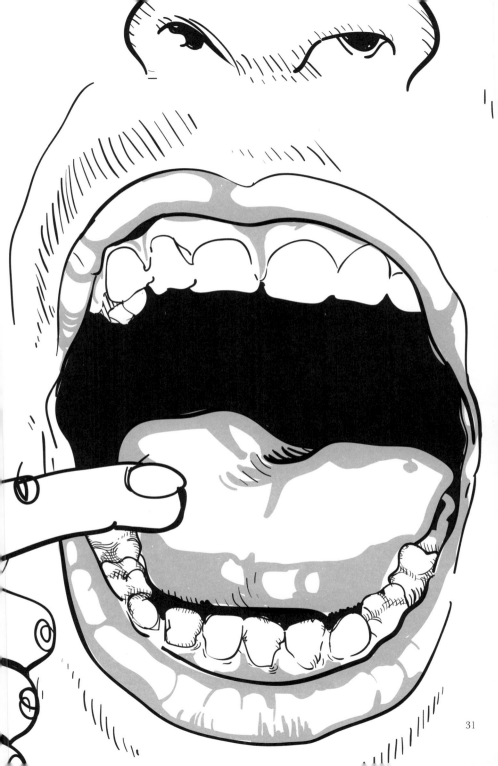

You'll offer him a couple of sandwiches from the old sheikh's fuul stand, but he'll eagerly suggest tasty burgers from 'Cook Toor' instead.

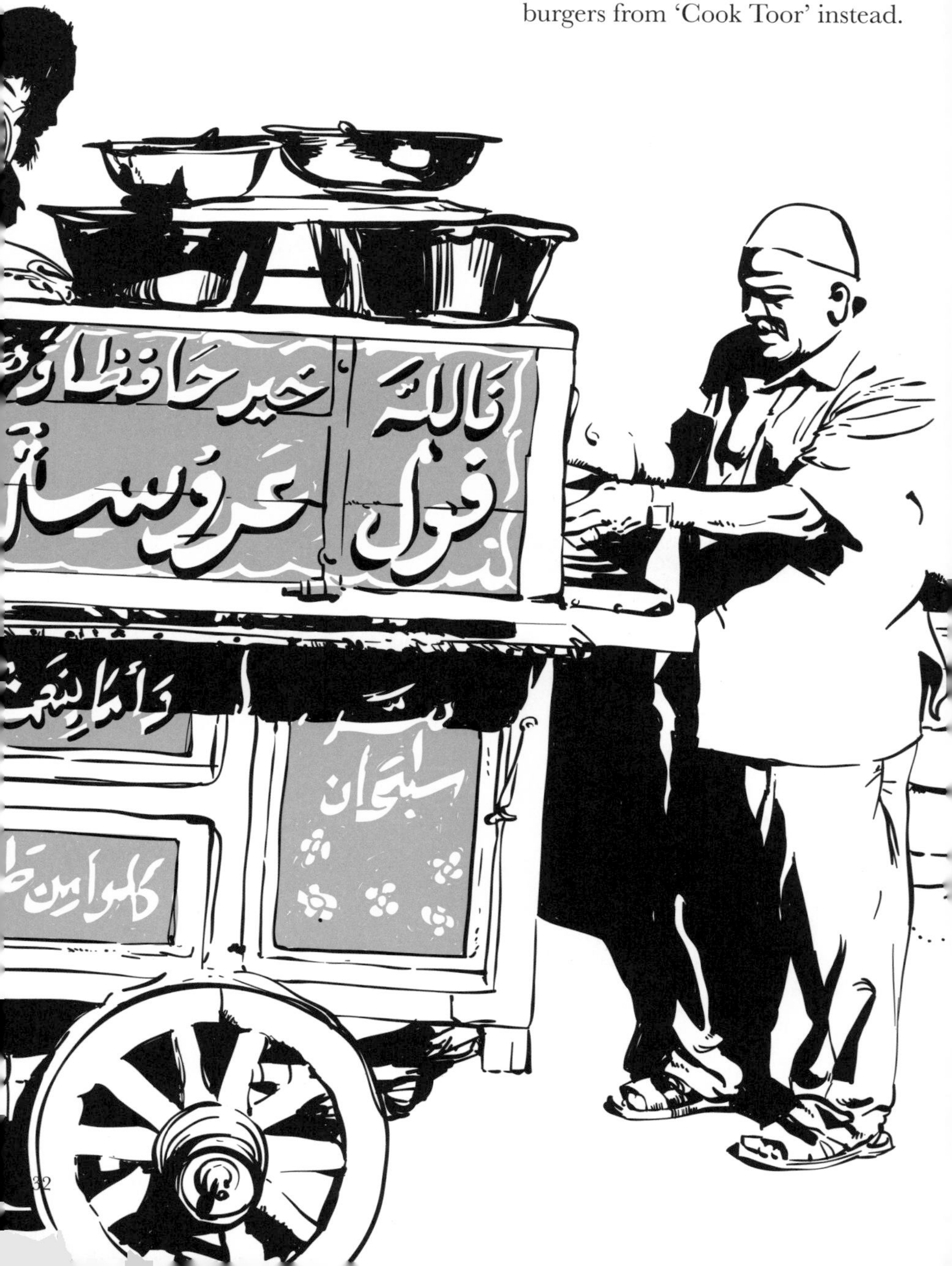

سبحان

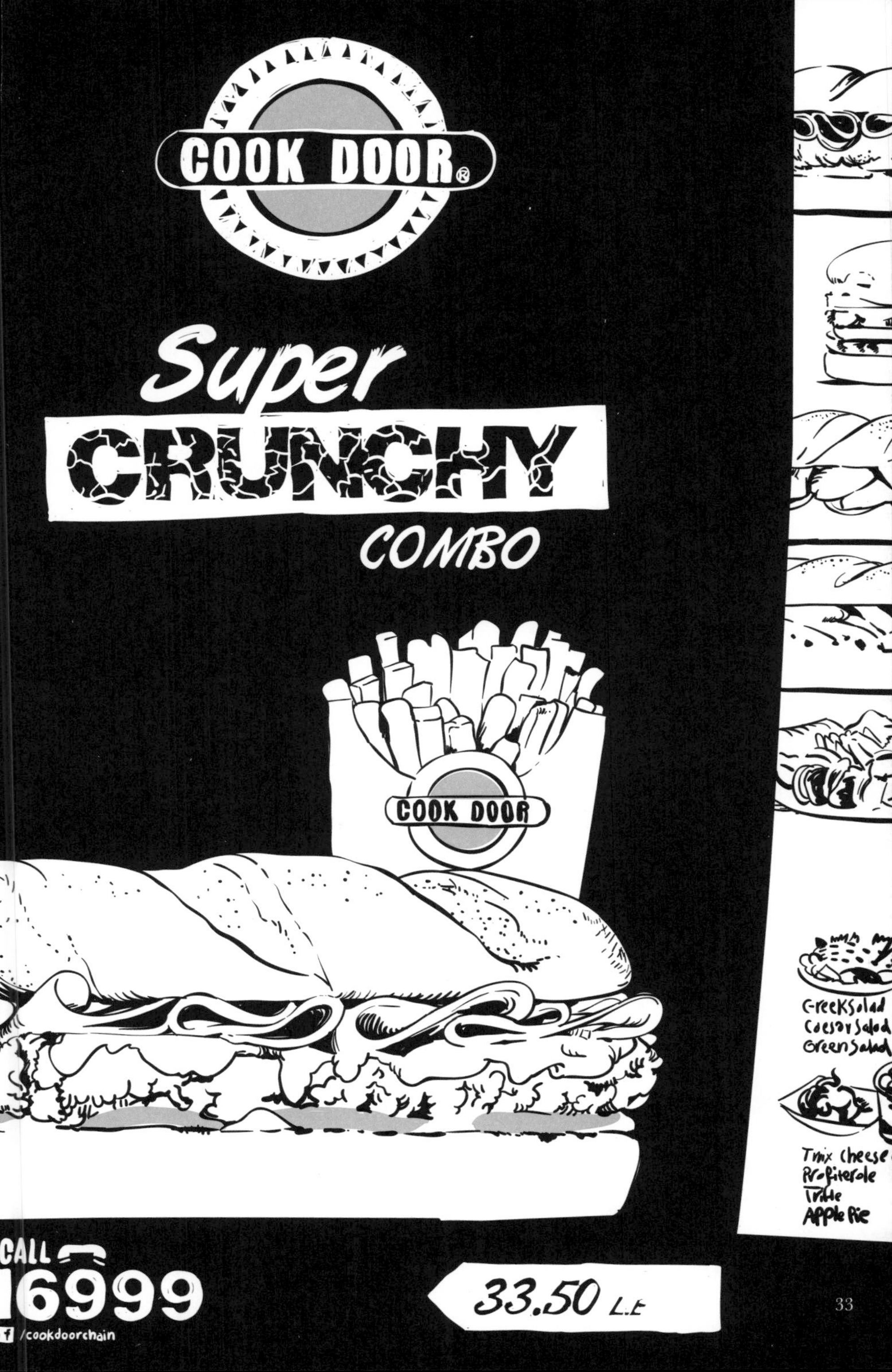
COOK DOOR
Super
CRUNCHY
COMBO
COOK DOOR
CALL
16999
/cookdoorchain
33.50 L.E
GreekSalad
CaesarSalad
GreenSalad
Twix cheese
Profiterole
Trifle
Apple Pie

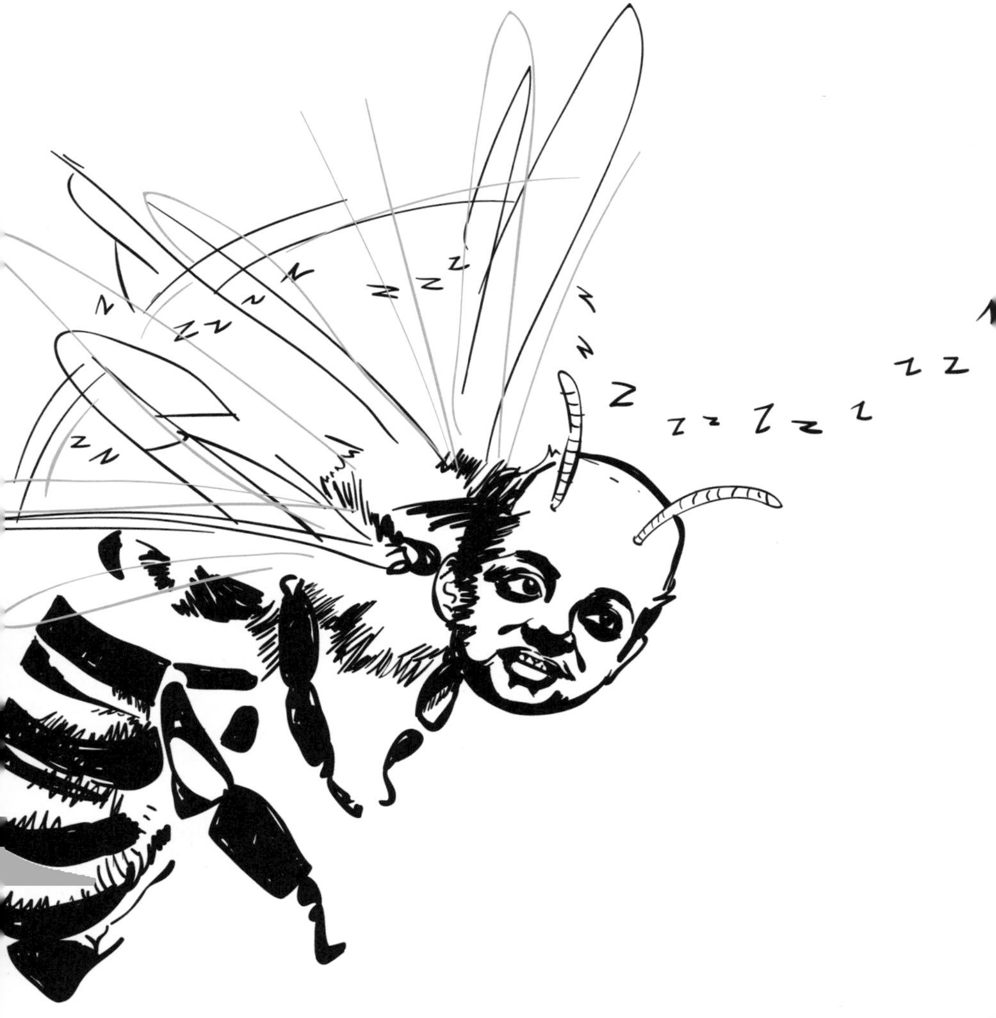

When you ignore him, he'll buzz around you, and then retreat beneath the shade of a ficus tree to sit next to a pair of siblings. The day before, the tree will have been stripped of all its leaves in a tyrannical pruning operation. The branches, still strewn across the concrete sidewalk, will trip Hamada as he rushes over to a kind-looking woman, and send him tumbling. Just before your heart goes out to him, you'll hear him cry:

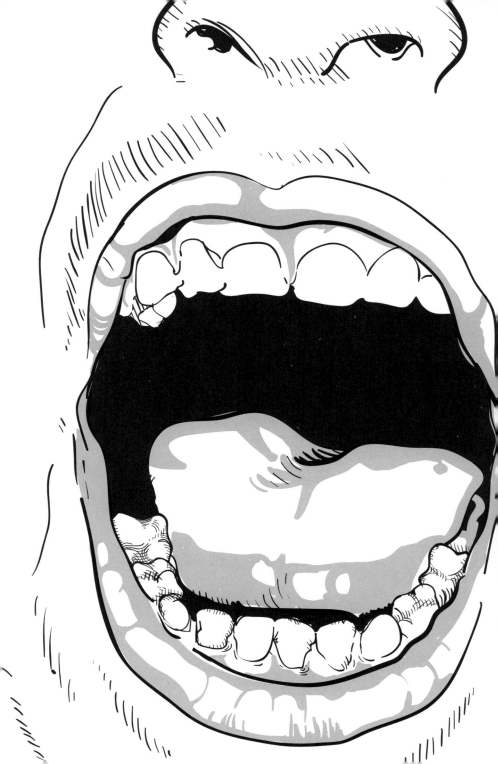

Mamaaaa!

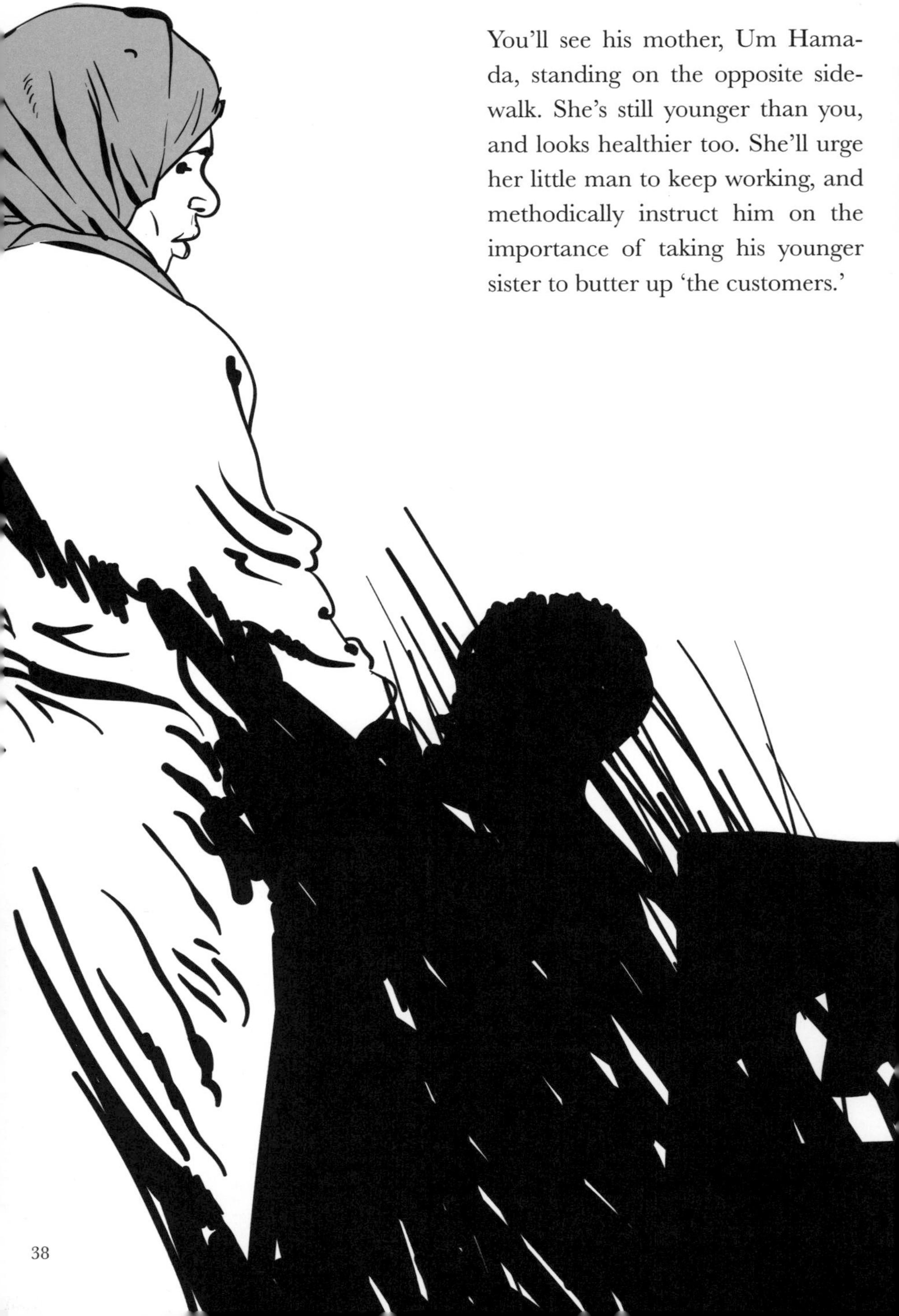

You'll see his mother, Um Hamada, standing on the opposite sidewalk. She's still younger than you, and looks healthier too. She'll urge her little man to keep working, and methodically instruct him on the importance of taking his younger sister to butter up 'the customers.'

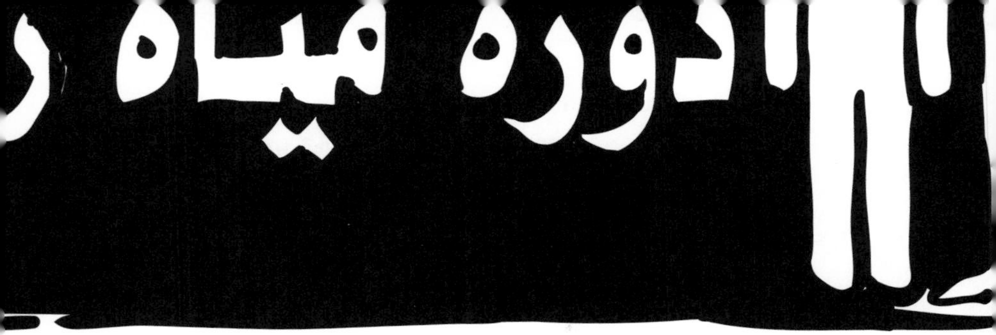
دورة مياه

Um Hamada will swiftly slip away and return to her headquarters by the public bathrooms in the parking lot, where the square's pungent smells and loiterers concentrate. Whenever you walk through Bab el-Louk, a six-year-old carrying a two-year-old will stop you to tell you that he's hungry.

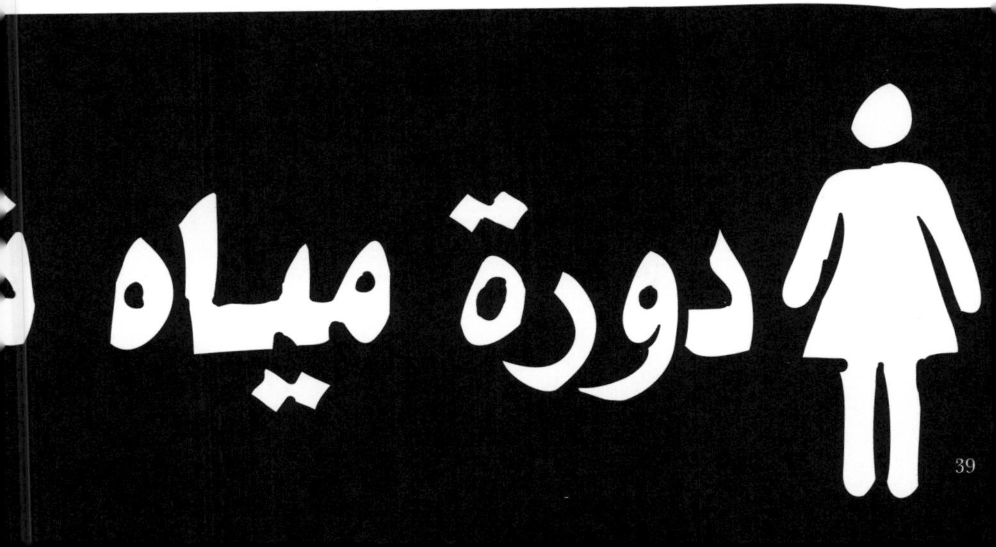
دورة مياه

You'll love writing on the walls of the apartment in Bab el-Louk, to the sound of the TV, always playing in the background.

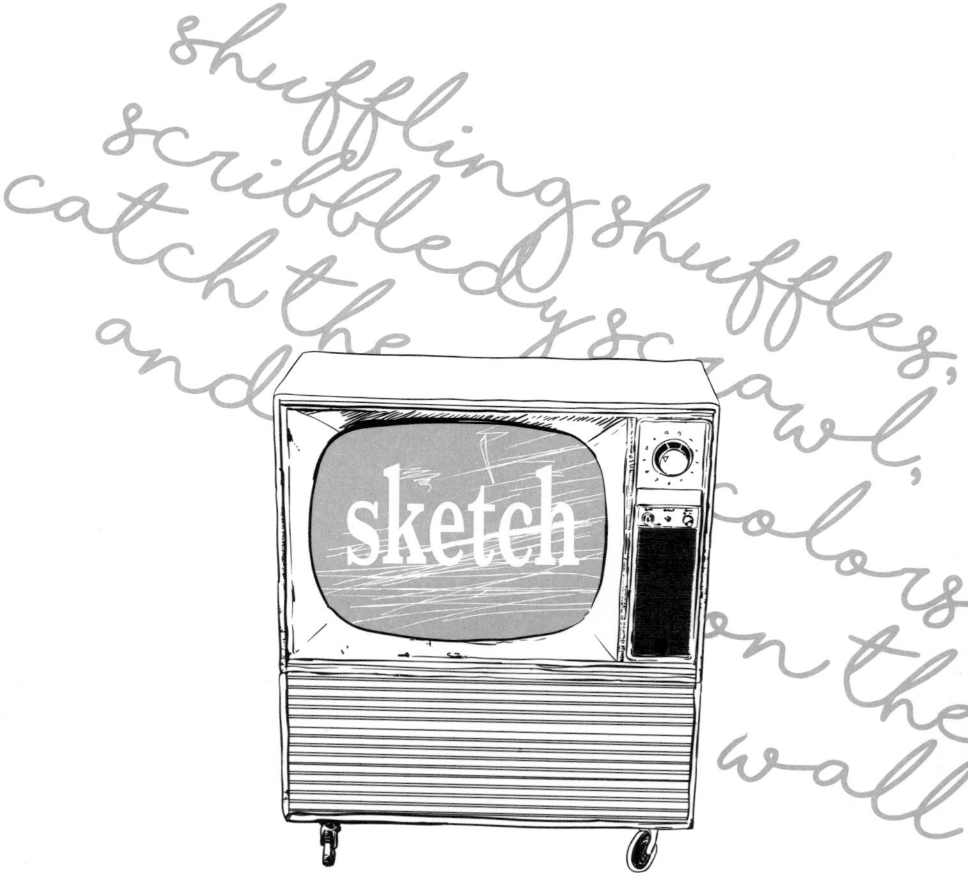
shuffling
shuffles;
scribbled
scrawl,
catch the
colors;
and
on the
wall
sketch

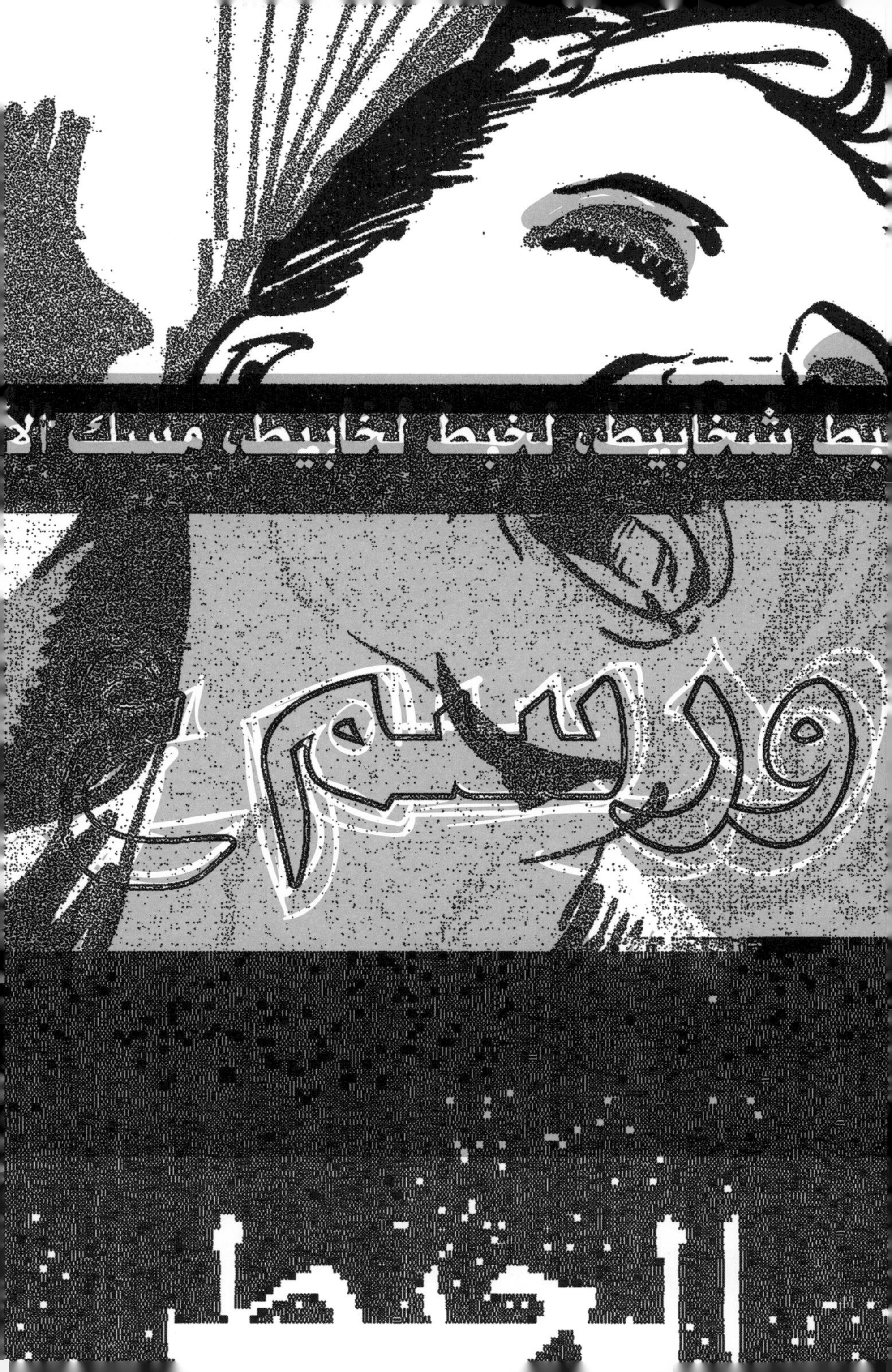
شخابيط، لخبط لخابيط، مسك
ورسم

Though you'll worry about the security deposit. You're constantly rearranging the furniture, but you can't find the right place for anything. It doesn't make sense: why won't the tools you organized only yesterday stay put?

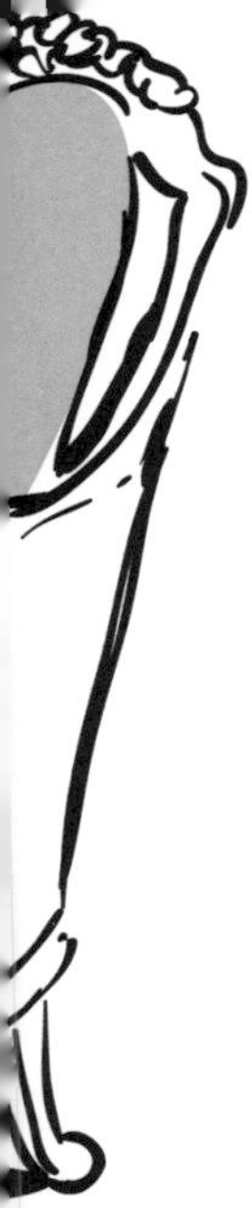

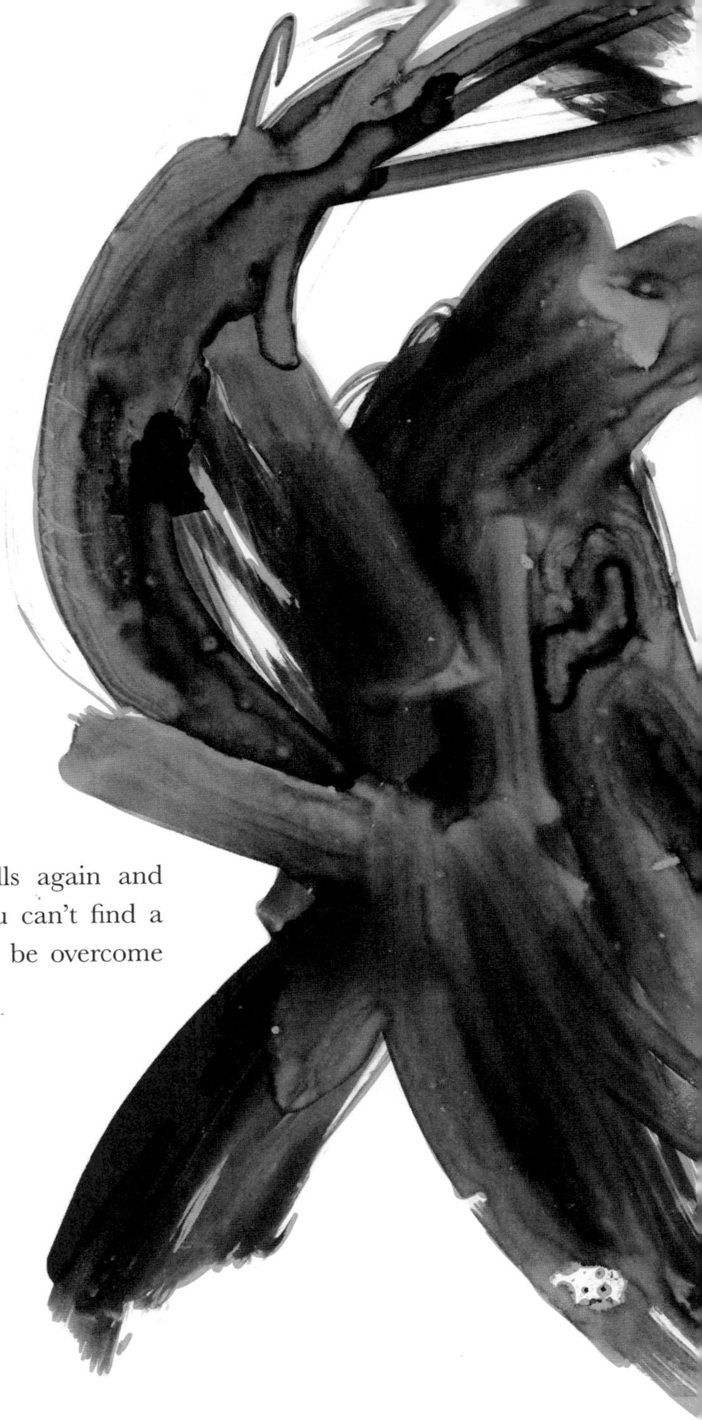

You'll paint the walls again and again, and when you can't find a suitable shade, you'll be overcome by paranoia.

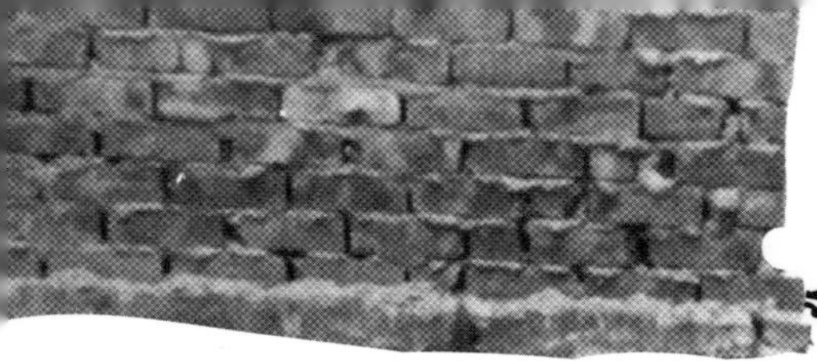

The man who collects money for the electricity bill hates you with a passion, and the old retired elevator ***clatters*** in protest when you force it to work.

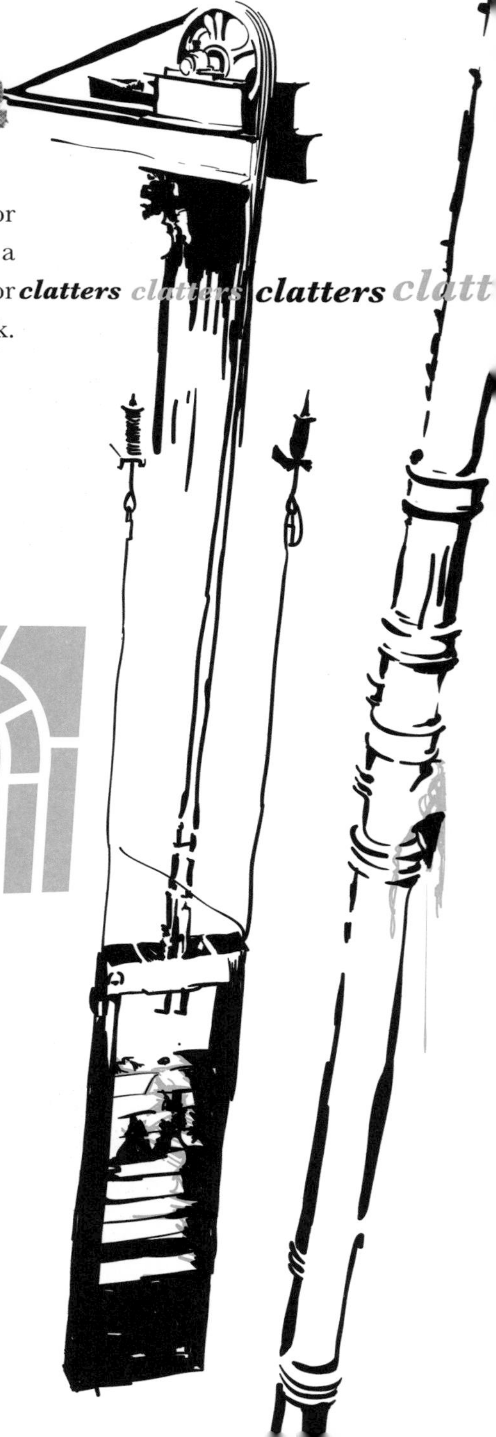
clatters clatters clatters clatt

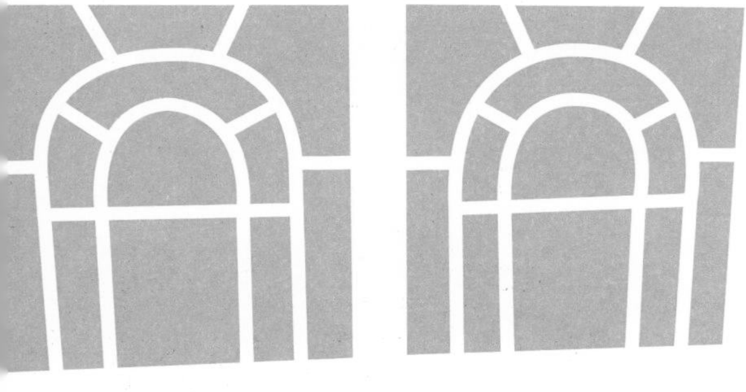

atters *clatters* **clatters** *cl*

In Taher Restaurant you'll set down your bags of fruit, and a bit later you'll start screaming, trying to convince the cashier to rejuvenate you with a chopped liver sandwich and an eggplant salad. Then suddenly, you'll be struck by the sight of an old man.

He's staring at you.

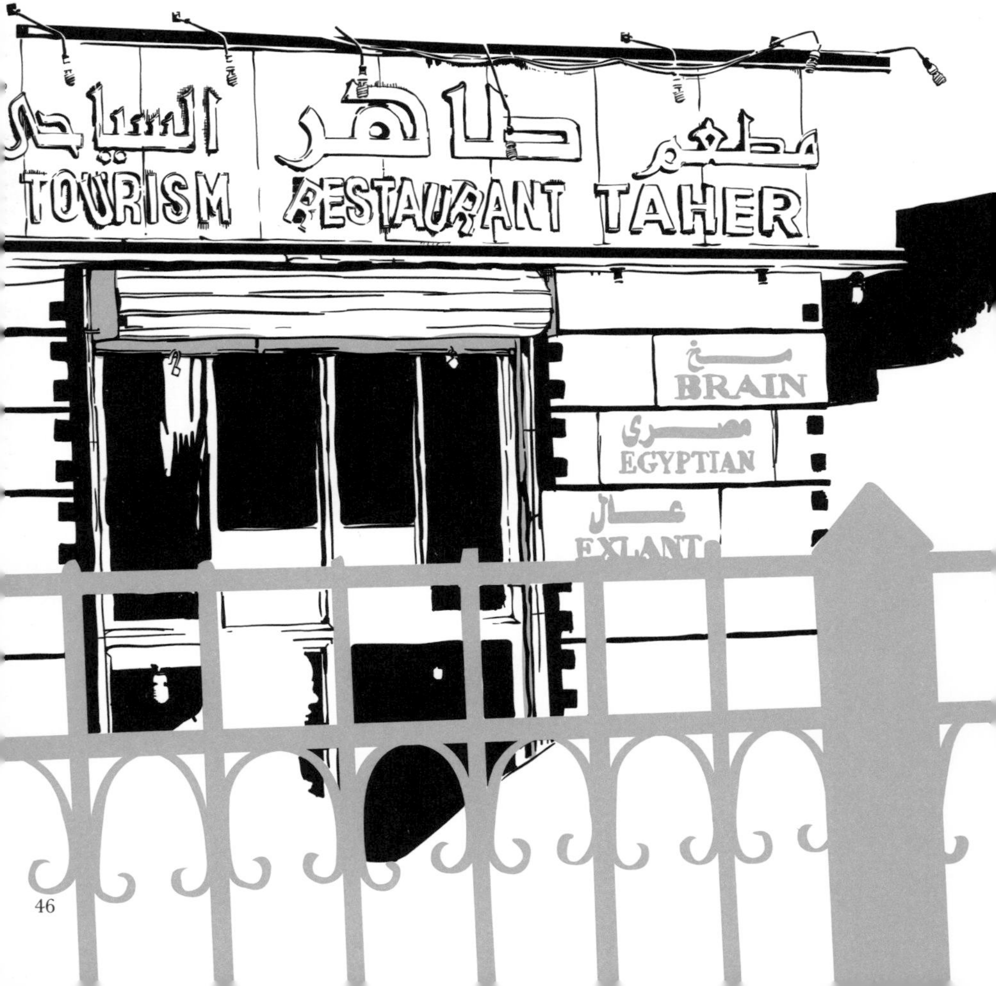

مطعم طاهر السياحي
TOURISM RESTAURANT TAHER
مخ
BRAIN
مصرى
EGYPTIAN
عال
EXLANT

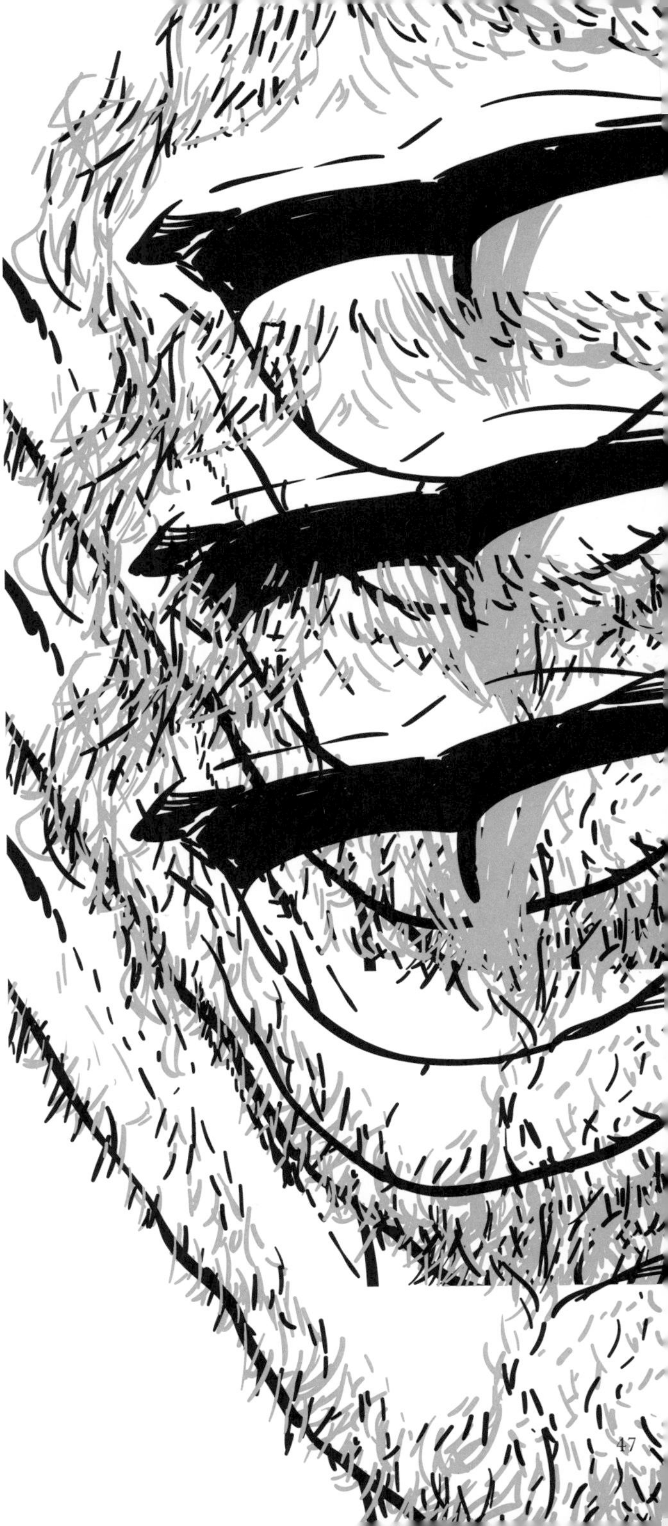

'You still standing?' He asks. A cynical laugh escapes his dark, toothless mouth. 'Hehehe.'

You take your garish plastic bag, and hear your retort emerge from the cashier's lips: 'God help you, old man.'

'Hehehe,' you laugh.

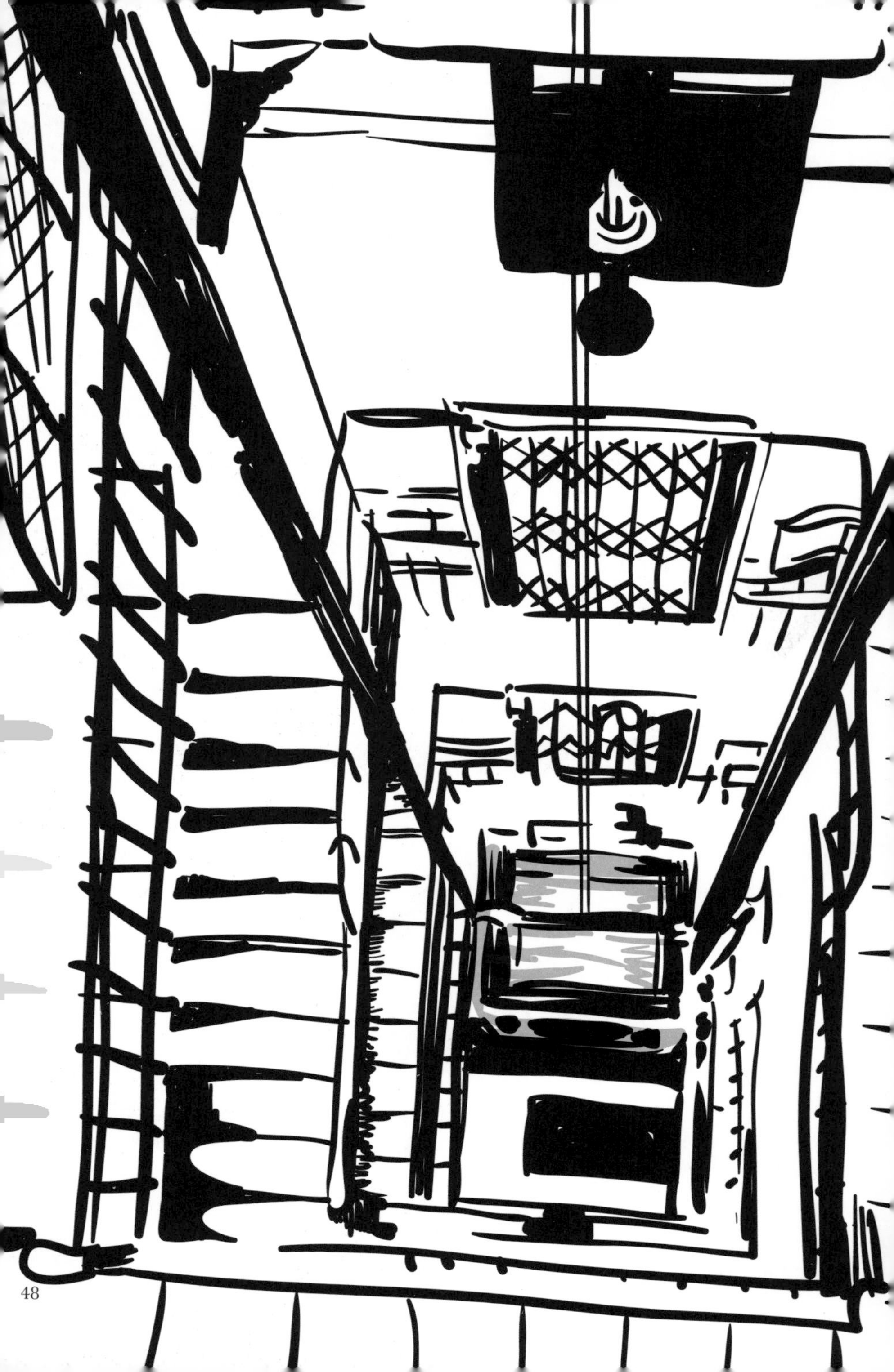

As you're turning the key in your apartment door – well aware the elevator is out of service – you'll realize you left a bag of fruit on the table back in the restaurant.

'Hehehe,' laughs Time.

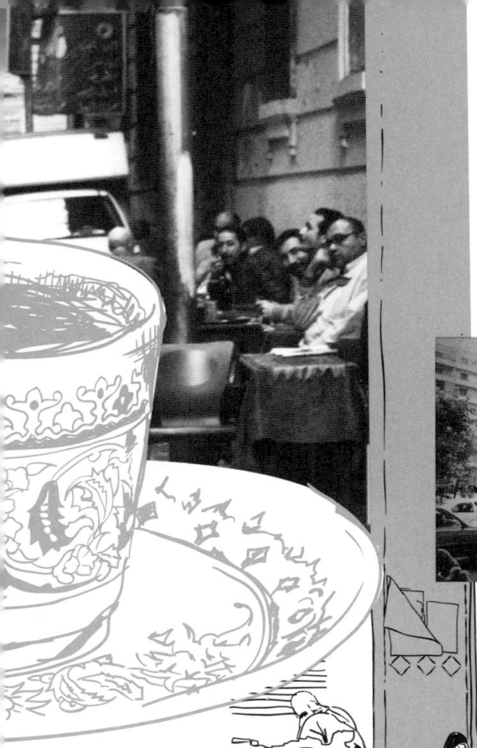

Below the apartment in Bab el-Louk are loads of bustling coffee-houses, and you'll often observe them from afar.

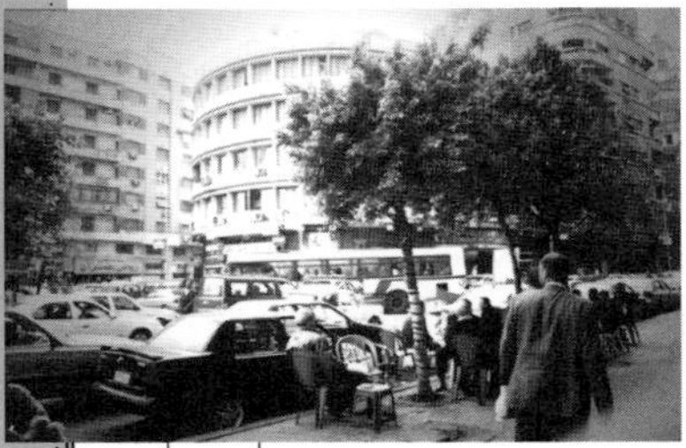

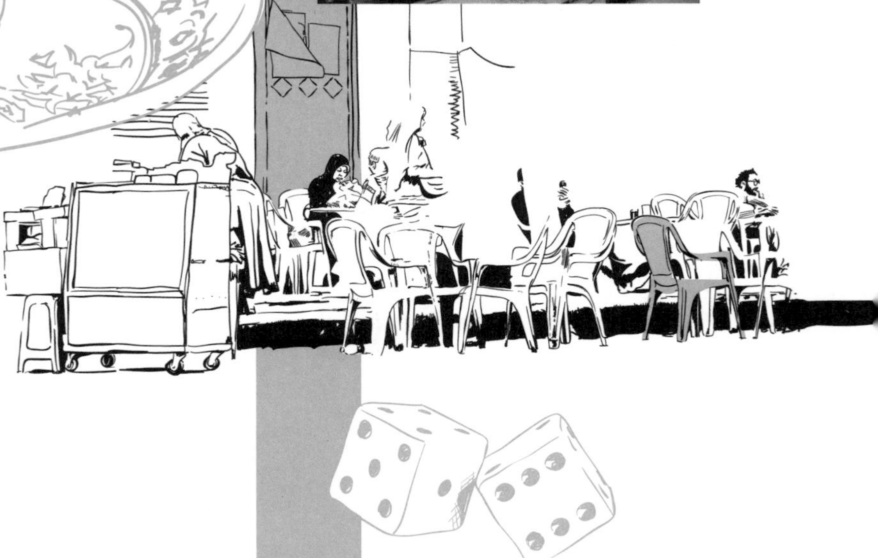

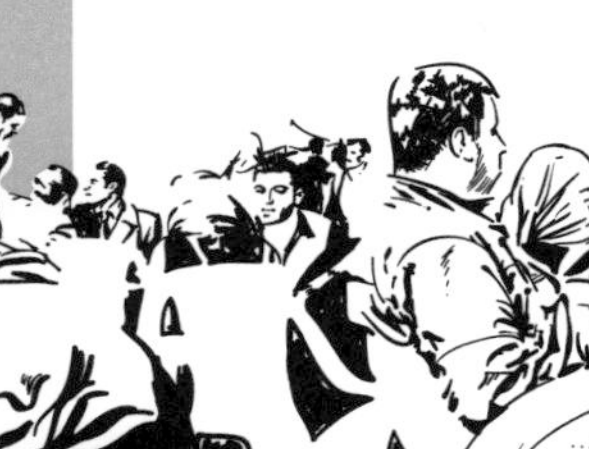

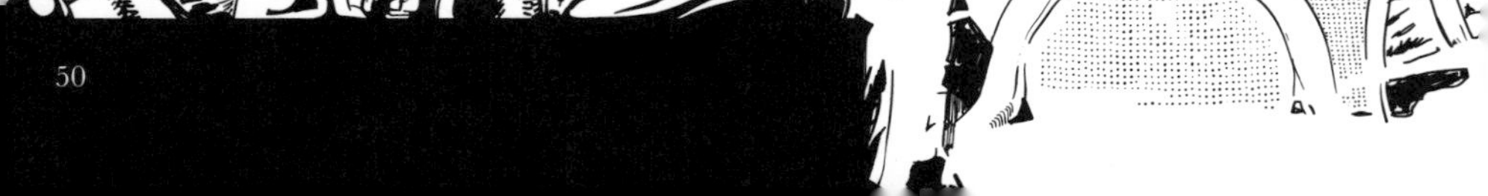

You'll decide to have coffee there tomorrow, but the days switch themselves up on you, as do the chairs, all while the people sitting there never change.

And still, you don't know for sure:
Do you take your coffee plain?

Or do you like it with a bit of sugar?

You could do all your shopping in the square below the apartment in Bab el-Louk, but you probably won't go out to buy a thing. 'Home delivery' will confine you to your chair, ruling over your lunch routine and the brand of toothpaste you use.

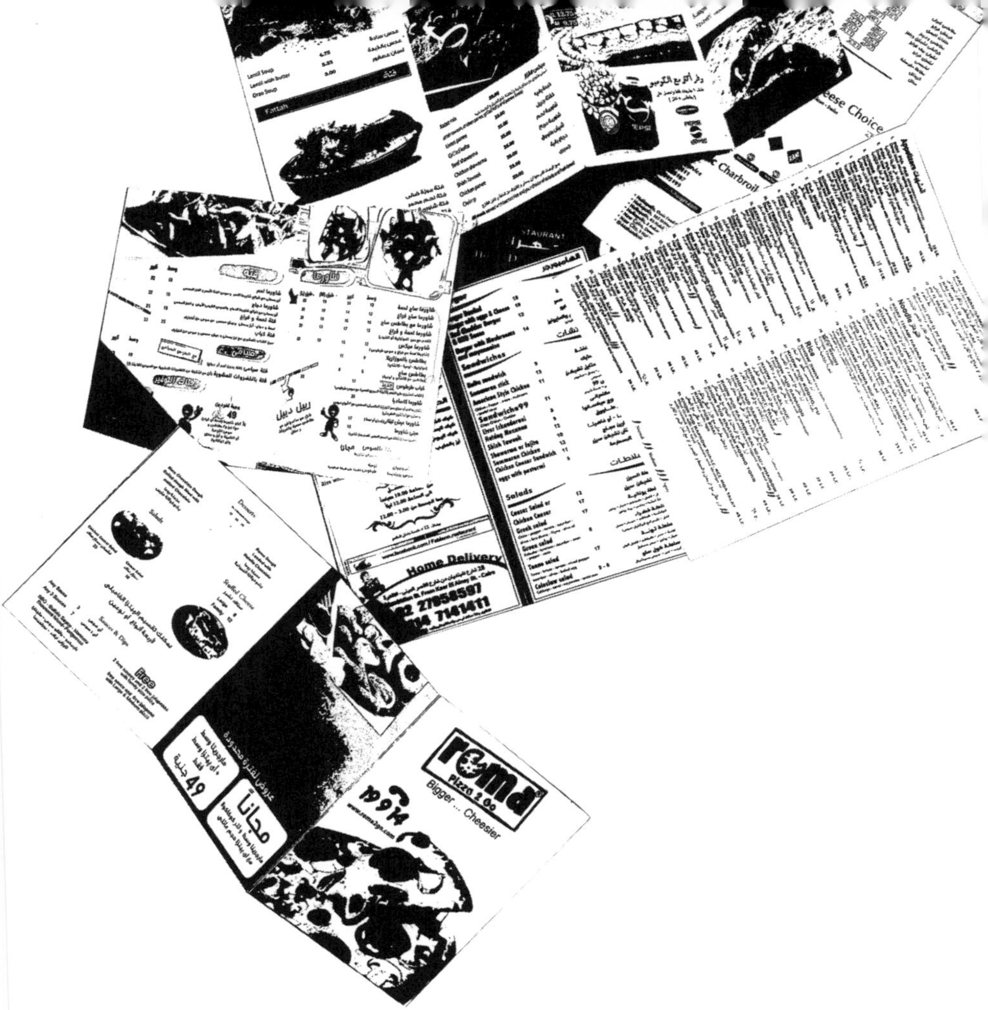
Lentil Soup
Lentil with butter
Orzo Soup
Fattah
Charbroil
Cheese Choice
Sandwiches
Salads
Home Delivery
roma
Pizza 2 Go
Bigger... Cheesier
www.roma2go.com
Desserts
Sauces & Dips
free

When you need a shirt from the market next door, the shopkeeper might ignore you or treat you gently, but either way you'll feel you're being swindled.

Your relationship with perfume shops and empty water bottles will deepen. You'll never catch sight of the man who collects your garbage, but you'll be woken daily by his shouting as he argues with the sleep-deprived soldiers in the square at dawn.

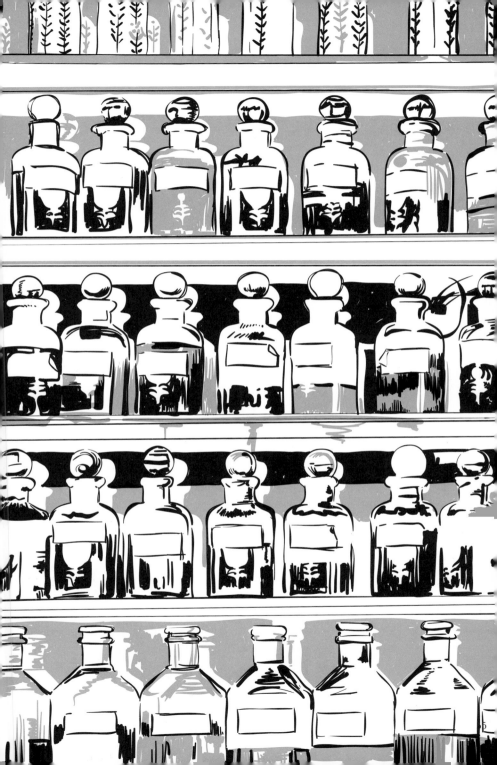

Central Security Force trucks will amass below your apartment in Bab el-Louk, signaling the presence of protests in Talaat Harb Square. You'll stand on your balcony, hear the chanting and think:

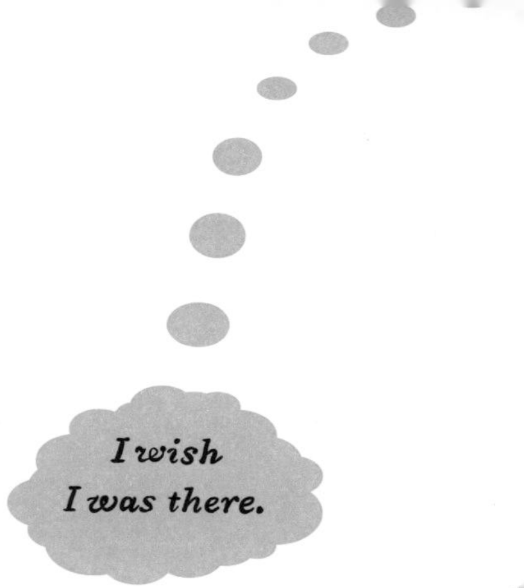
I wish
I was there.

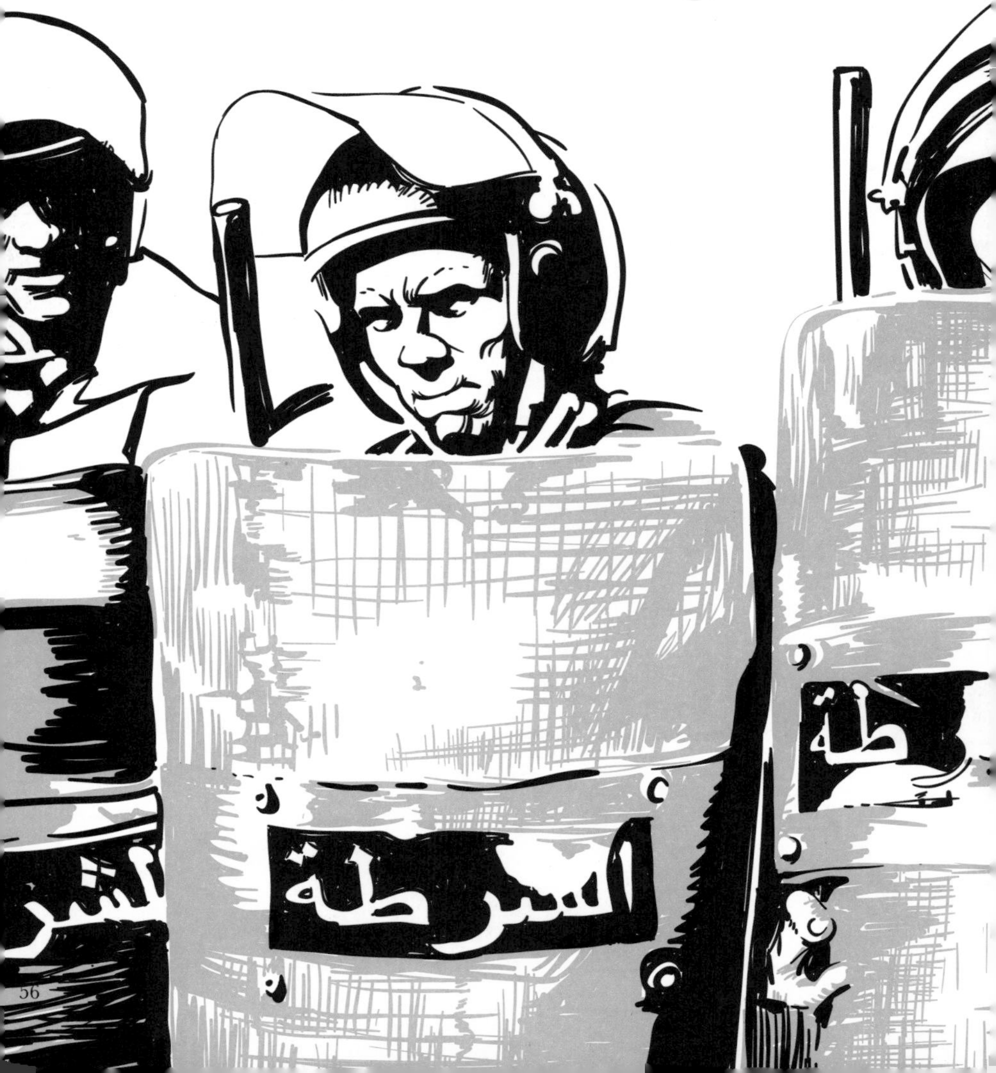
الشرطة

You'll be filled with empathy, eventually, and decide that you're:

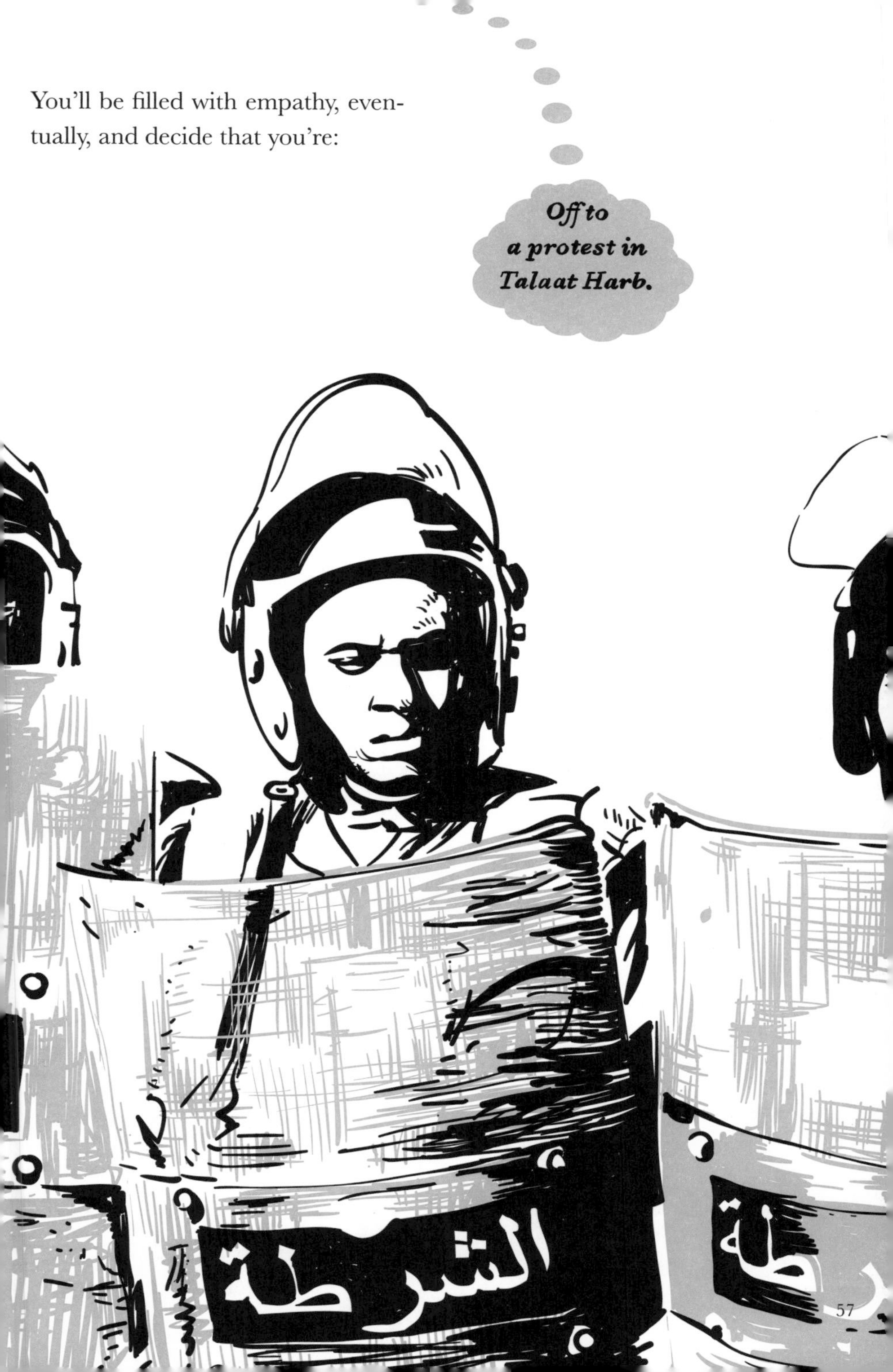
Off to
a protest in
Talaat Harb.
الشرطة
طة

You'll walk around the square for two hours, hearing protesters but never seeing them. You'll want to stand there for a moment, but someone next to you will tell you to move along.

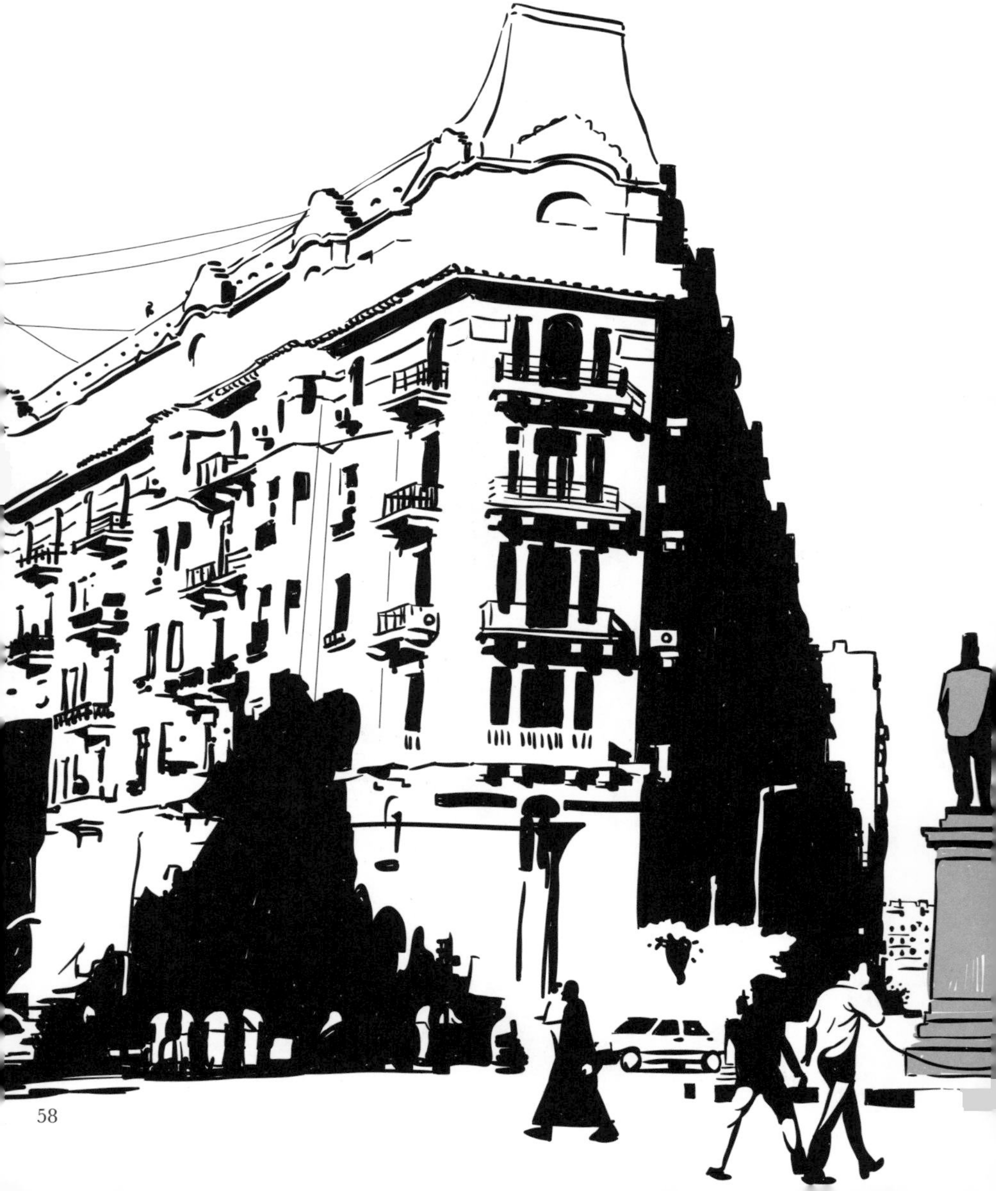

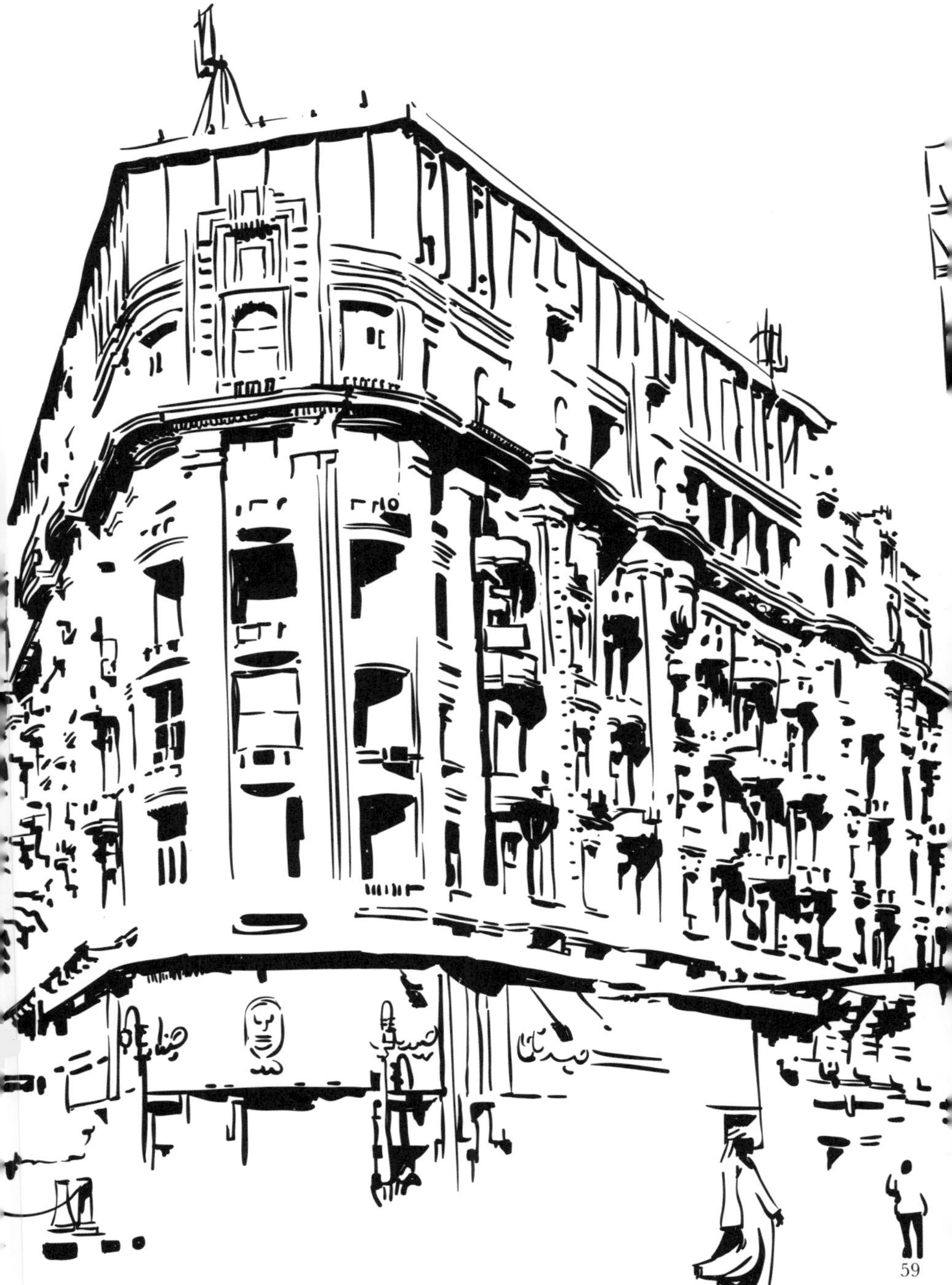

Twice each day, while you're glued to the television, you'll hear a caravan of barking dogs, at half past eleven in the morning and half ten at night.

You'll never figure out whether it's a hard-of-hearing fan, obsessed with a soap opera rerun, or a ruthless man on a nightly outing with his strange pack. But you'll keep on wondering.

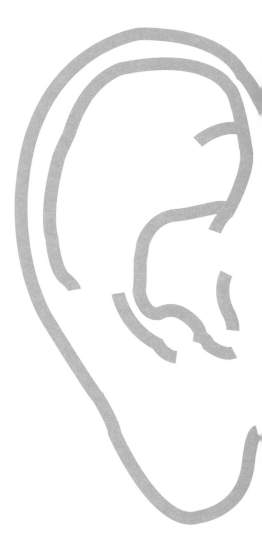

In the apartment in Bab el-Louk, on the morning of the presidential elections, you'll be assailed by cars with megaphones on top and 'Government' written on the side. Hours before the results are announced, you'll hear:

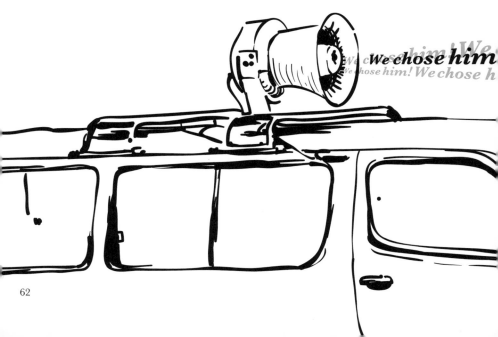

We chose him! We chose him! We chose him!

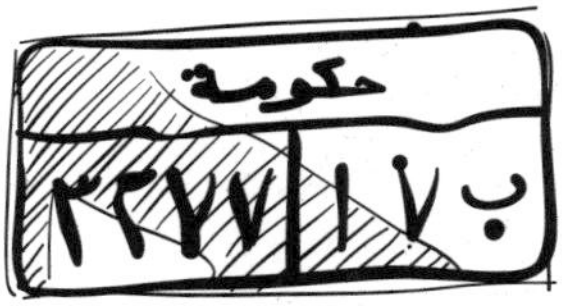
حكومة
٣٤٧٧
١٧ ب

him! Day after day, our hea

chose him! Day after day,

y after day, our hearts are with him

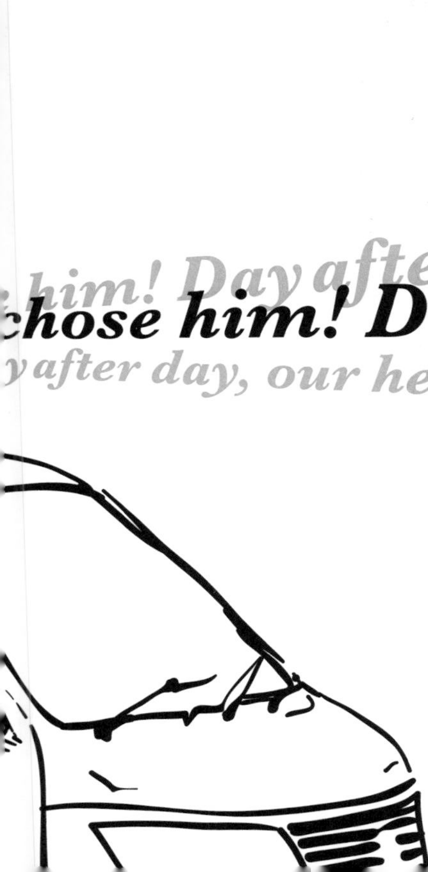

You won't understand who they're referring to. Even so, you'll sing snippets of the song, in tune with the departing cars as they cut across the square.

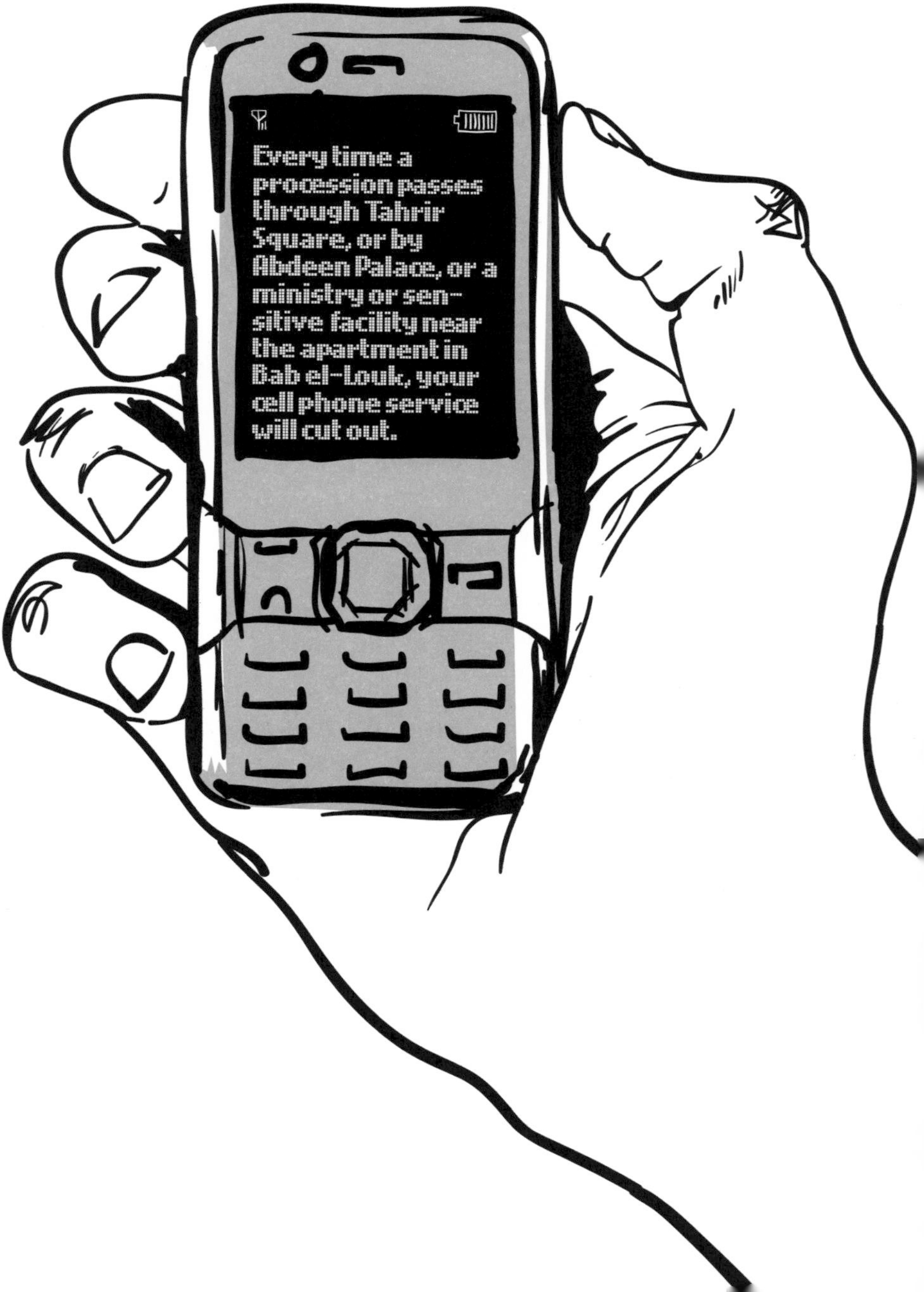
Every time a procession passes through Tahrir Square, or by Abdeen Palace, or a ministry or sen-sitive facility near the apartment in Bab el-Louk, your cell phone service will cut out.

On the roof across from your bedroom window, you discover a Nubian family. One of them sleeps outside – summer or winter, in a tent of used blankets – while the rest of the girls (you're unsure how many there are) sleep in two rooms built of bricks and old junk. You'll hear their screaming matches on weekends and holidays. You'll count at least a dozen people in that small spot on top of the building.

On a neighboring roof, another family takes good care of their plants, and one of them has a huge faux Pharaonic statue. If you lean a little to the left, you'll be able to see its nose, and through their window you'll spy a table with assorted odds and ends: graph ruled sketch pads (one of the girls is definitely an art student), plastic bags (you have plenty too, they're useful for storing things), a box of watercolors whose poor quality you tested out yourself, a small cassette player missing its lid, and some tapes, most of which feature singers you don't care for.

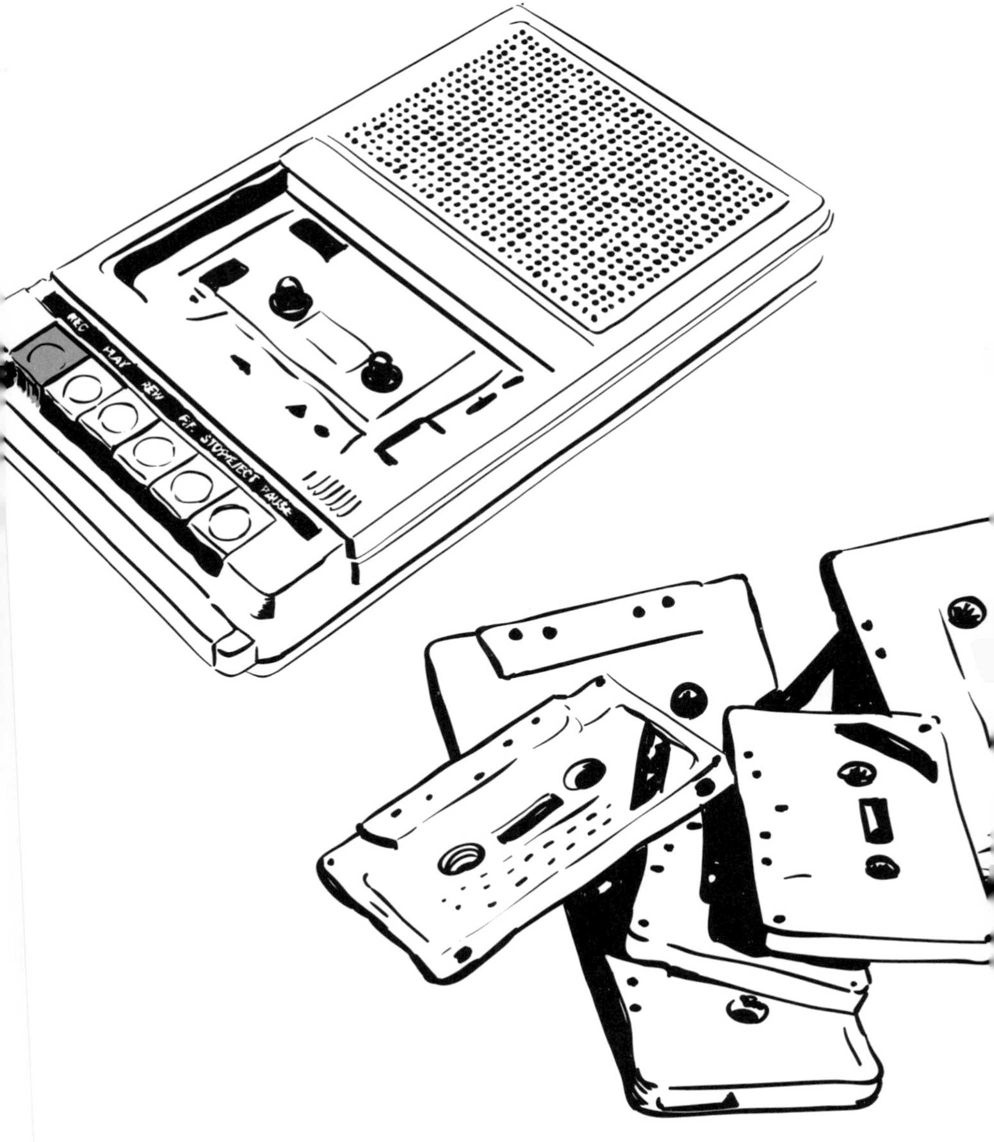
REC
PLAY
REW
F.F.
STOP/EJECT
PAUSE

From inside the apartment in Bab el-Louk, you excel in the art of snooping.

EVERY TIME YOU READ THE MORNING PAPER

You'll begin with the crime section. You'll always peruse it in the afternoon. By then it's not worth reading, since a few hours after news breaks it's no longer news. Events begin their life as happenstance, and end as hearsay. These days you ask God to forgive your wicked uncle like someone mentioning a saint, so allow me:

'Was he a saint?'
'Don't you think so?'
'Are you a saint?'
'Don't you think so?'

No, no, your uncle's deeds don't dwell in the past, they've become purely legend, no longer fresh. They're probably rotting with him in his grave, or – if you have faith in your heart – he's being judged for them. We don't forgive the dead

because we're better than them, but because they're gone from the material world, where we can take our revenge and set fire to their behinds, or their cheeks if your imagination is shy. His wicked words and deeds are insubstantial now, they've turned into tales. You don't understand me anymore? Well then

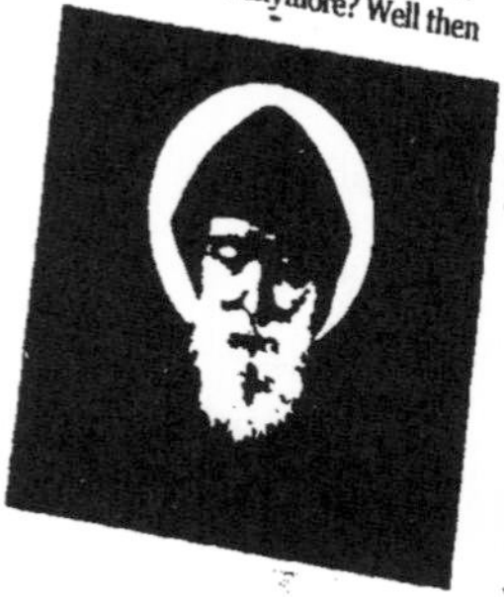

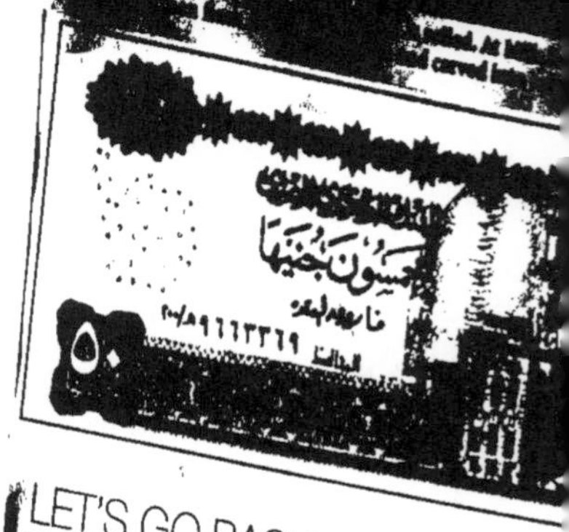

LET'S GO BACK TO

YOU SITTING IN THE APARTMENT IN BAB EL-LOUK

Your cup of coffee and a two week old crime section. You read:

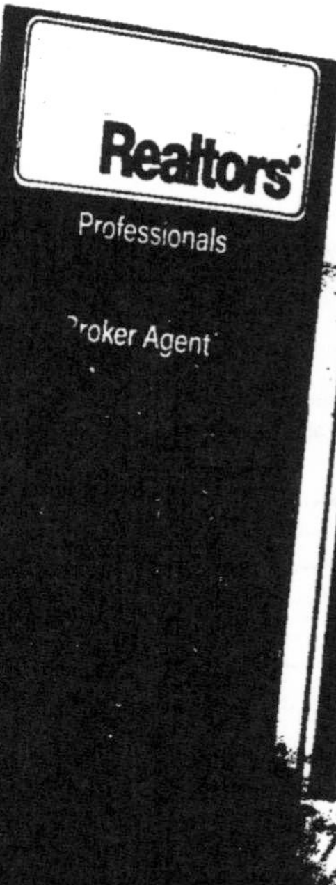

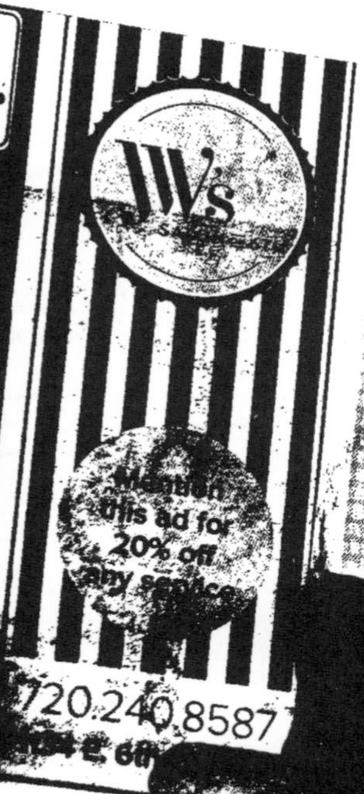
JW's
Mention this ad for 20% off any service
720.240.8587

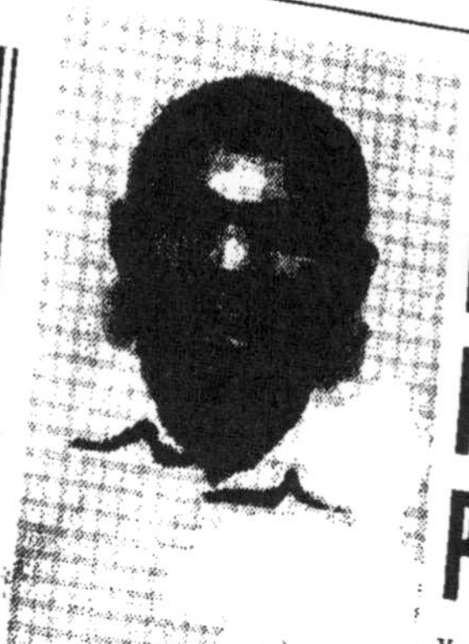

A MAN KIL HIS BROTH FOR FIFTY POUNDS

You shake with laughter, imag the family's situation, one sibli kills the other for… for… ha h …all for ha ha ha… fifty… ha haa

Jay DeRose of ... already looking for ... -roasted beans. The roaster ...

you can't try most of the ... buy. Sizes run from ... to men's 14s and 15s ...

In addition to ... Vices sells ... toys. ... The C... ... for ... your luck and ... a pair of pricey footwear.

Vices' graphic designer Maurice Anderson told LIFE the new store is sponsoring a school supply drive dubbed 'Bigger Than Shoes' that will run until August 11. Every donation earns a raffle ticket for a drawing during the 'Big Give-away' celebration on August 12 from noon-4:00p.m. when area youth can get free backpacks and school supplies. Free street ... also part of the party. A decidedly impressive way to launch a unique business. Check it out.

Latin Ameri... driving down ... The ... media KT... swinging north to ... the shuttle ... evenings ... Mourtada. ... will be ... begin. Look for the sandwich ...

YOU FLIP ONTO YOUR BACK

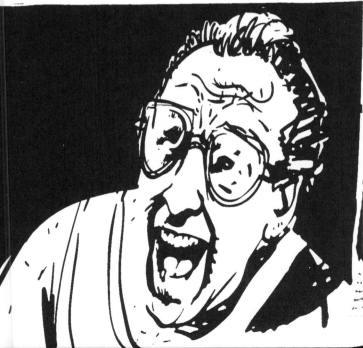

With tears in your eyes as you roll over, imagining his mother saying: my son murdered my son, ha ha he hee hee. You're afraid you'll die of laughter right here, ha ha haaaa he laughter right here, ha ha haaaa heh heh haaa heh haaa ha ha haaaa heh heh haaa

HA HA HAAAA HEH HEHHEHE HAAA HAAAAA

Ha ha haaaa heh heh haaa ha ha haaaa heh heh haaa ha ha haaaa he heh haaa ha ha haaaa heh heh haaa ha ha haaaa heh heh haaa ha ha haaaa heh heh haaa ha ha haaaa he heh haaa ha ha haaaa heh heh haa ha ha haaaa heh heh haaa ha ha haaaa heh heh haaa ha ha haaaa he heh haaa ha ha haaaa heh heh haaa ha ha haaaa heh heh haaa ha ha haaaa heh heh haaa ha ha haaaa he heh haaa ha ha haaaa heh heh haa ha ha haaaa heh heh haaa ha ha haaaa heh heh haaa

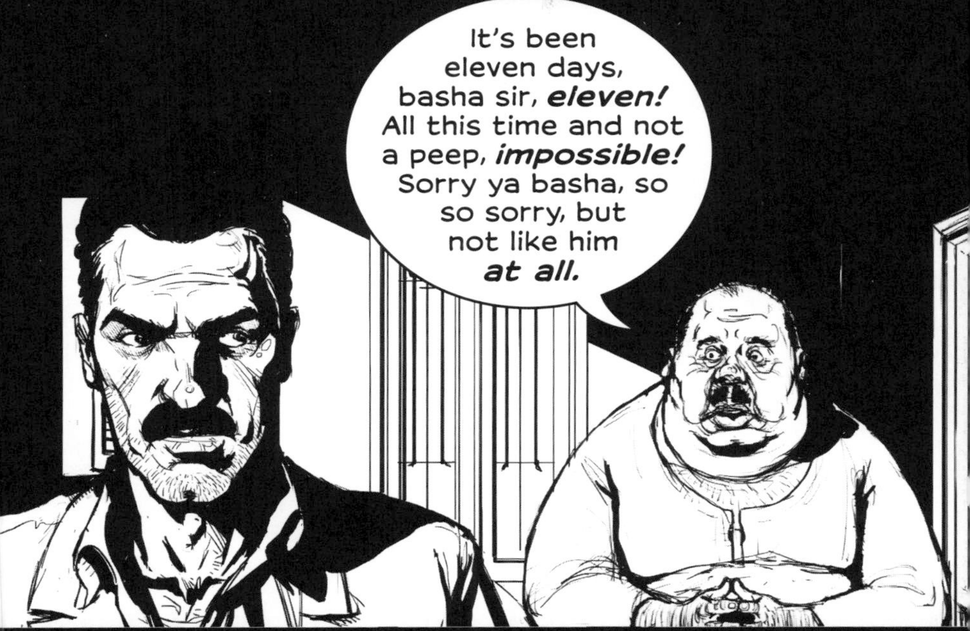
It's been eleven days, basha sir, *eleven!* All this time and not a peep, *impossible!* Sorry ya basha, so so sorry, but not like him *at all.*

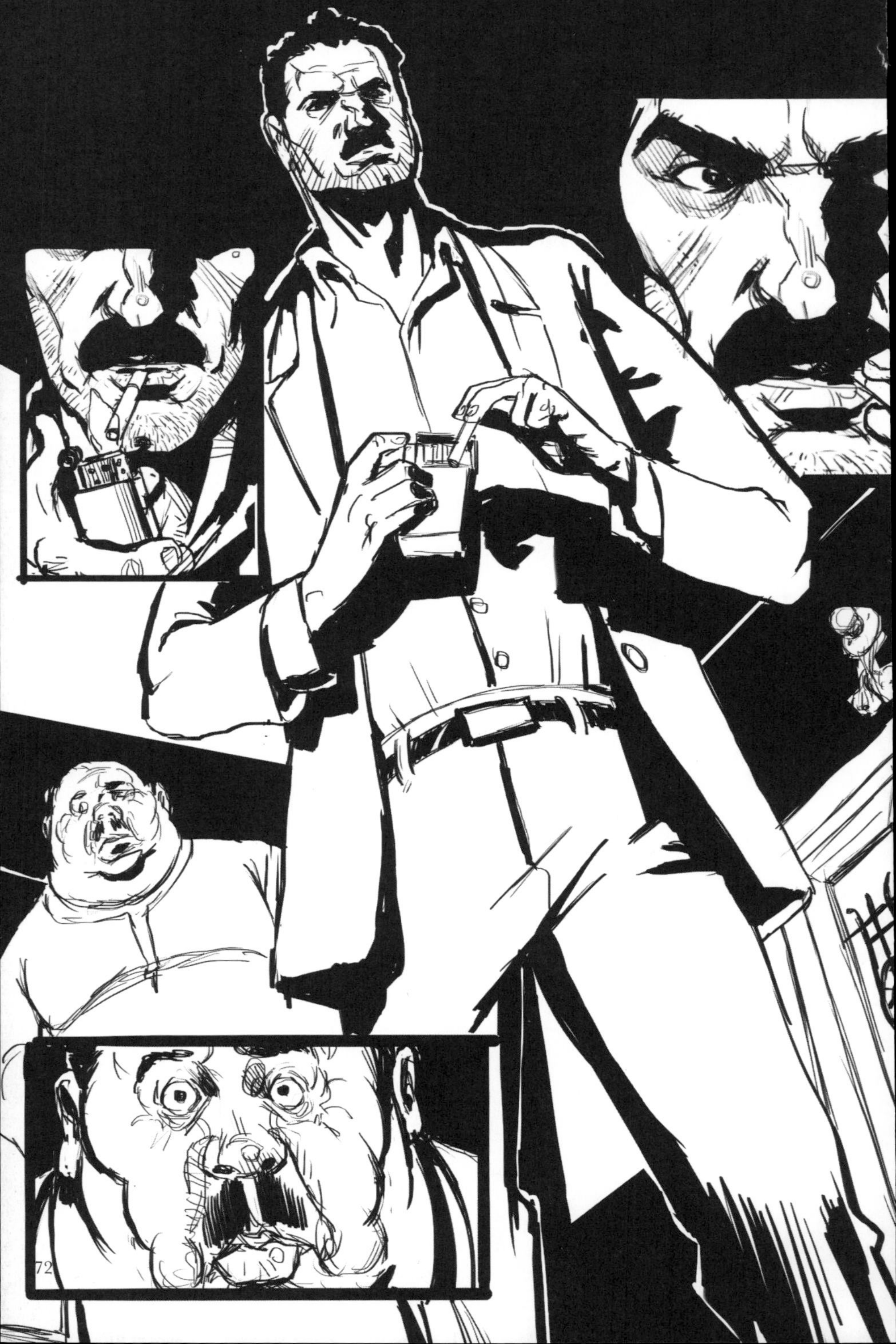

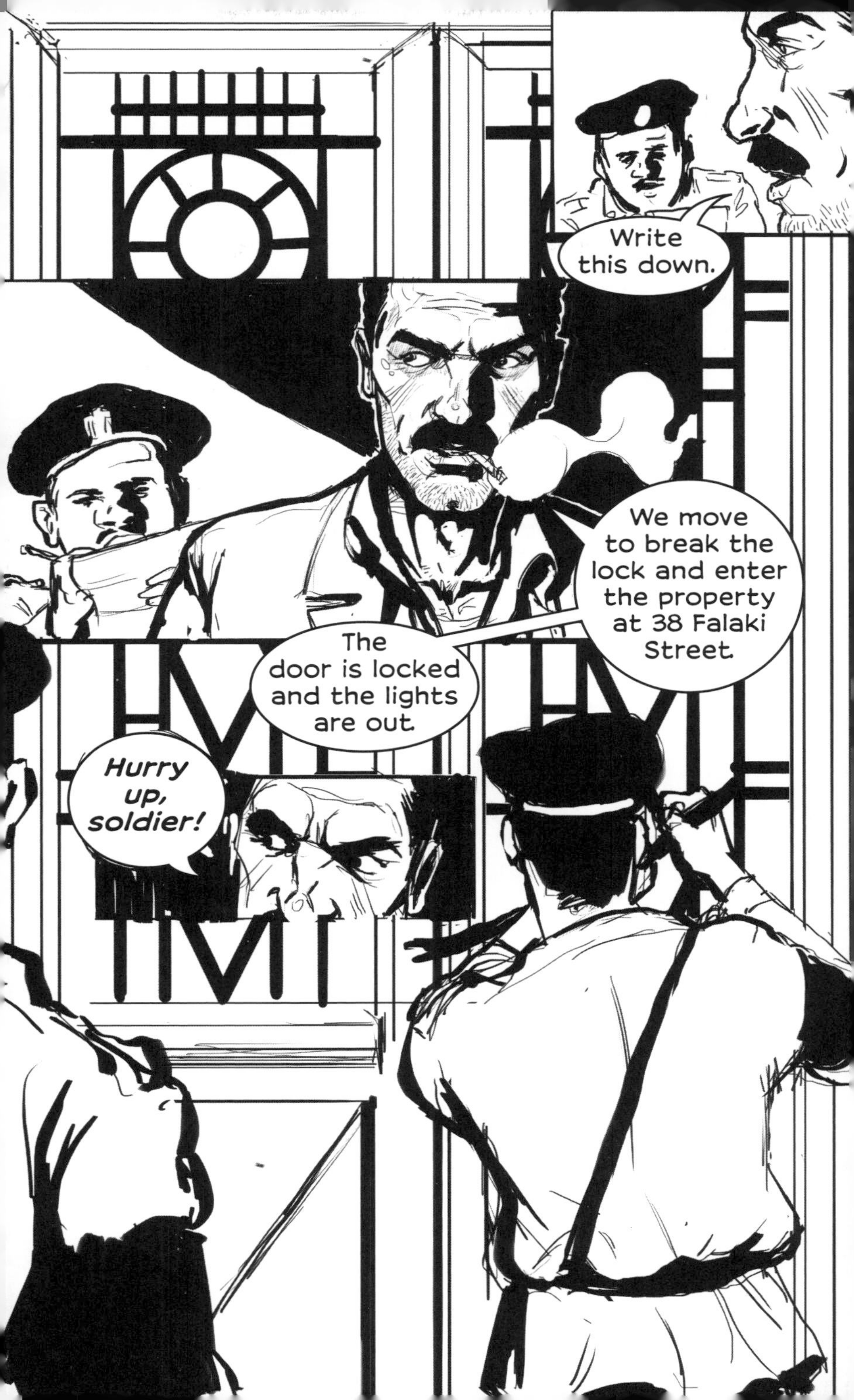
Write this down.
We move to break the lock and enter the property at 38 Falaki Street.
The door is locked and the lights are out.
Hurry up, soldier!

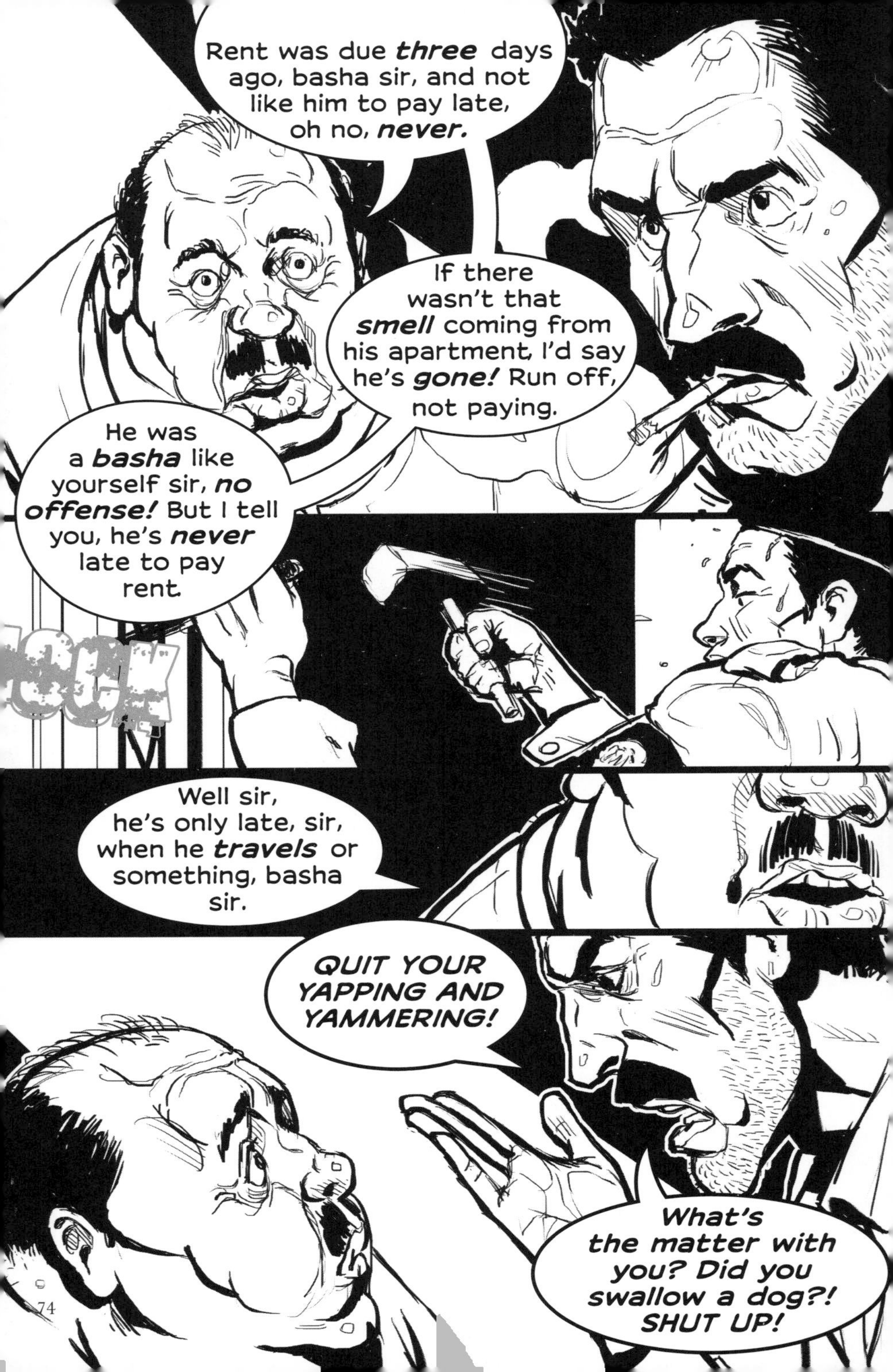
Rent was due *three* days ago, basha sir, and not like him to pay late, oh no, *never.*
If there wasn't that *smell* coming from his apartment, I'd say he's *gone!* Run off, not paying.
He was a *basha* like yourself sir, *no offense!* But I tell you, he's *never* late to pay rent.
Well sir, he's only late, sir, when he *travels* or something, basha sir.
QUIT YOUR YAPPING AND YAMMERING!
What's the matter with you? Did you swallow a dog?! SHUT UP!

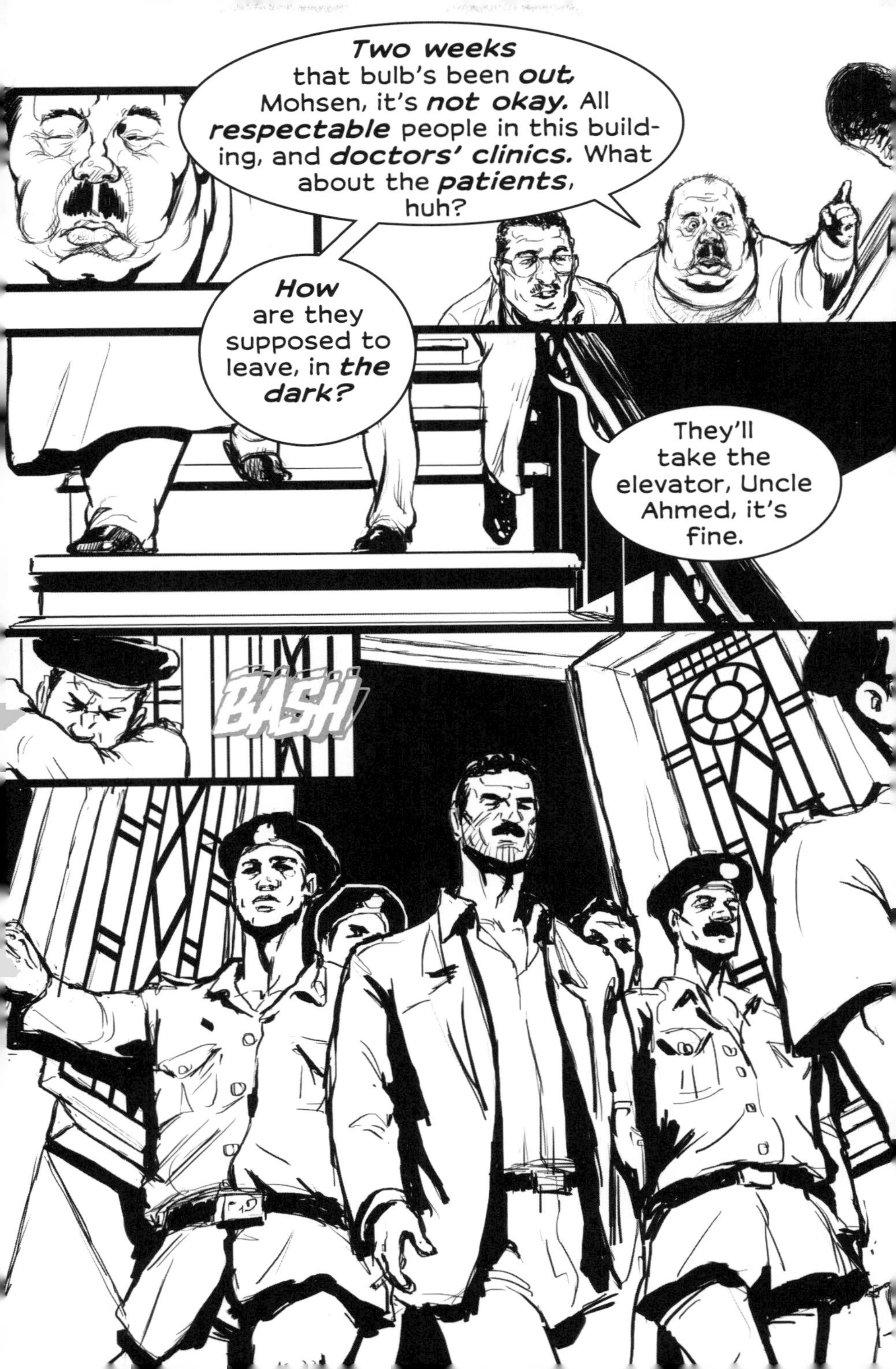

Two weeks that bulb's been out, Mohsen, it's not okay. All respectable people in this building, and doctors' clinics. What about the patients, huh?
How are they supposed to leave, in the dark?
They'll take the elevator, Uncle Ahmed, it's fine.
BASH!

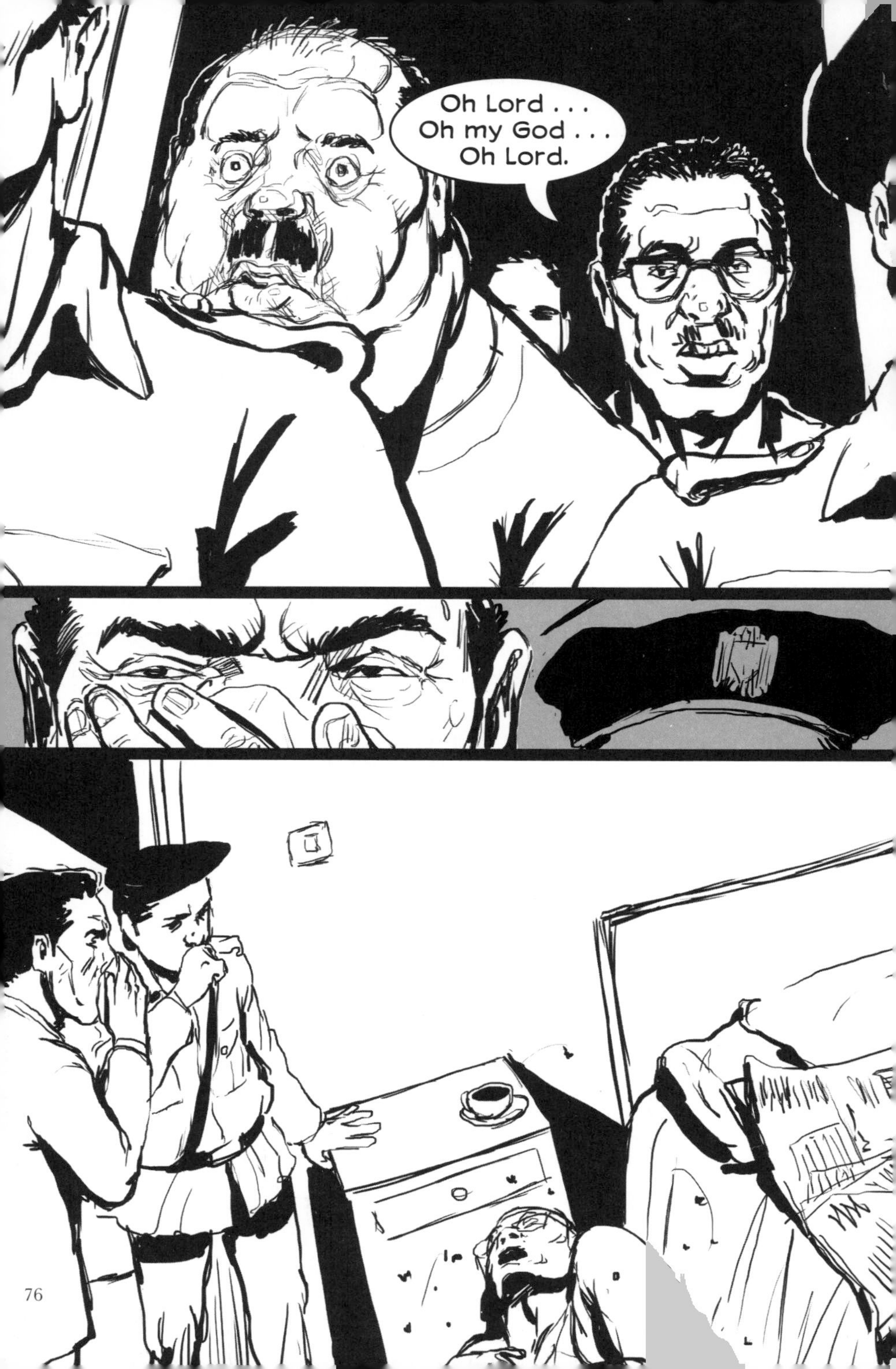
Oh Lord . . .
Oh my God . . .
Oh Lord.

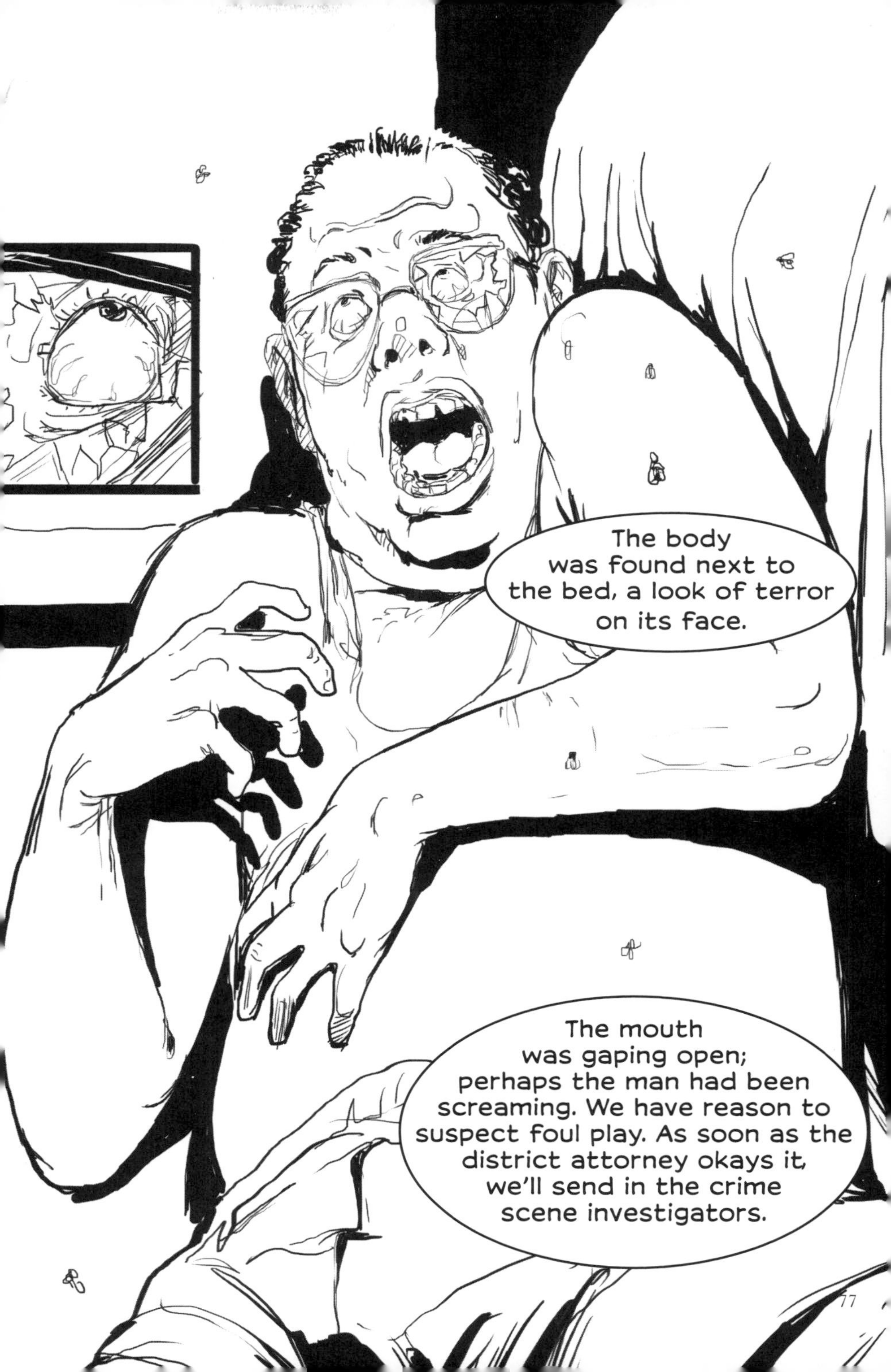
The body was found next to the bed, a look of terror on its face.
The mouth was gaping open; perhaps the man had been screaming. We have reason to suspect foul play. As soon as the district attorney okays it, we'll send in the crime scene investigators.

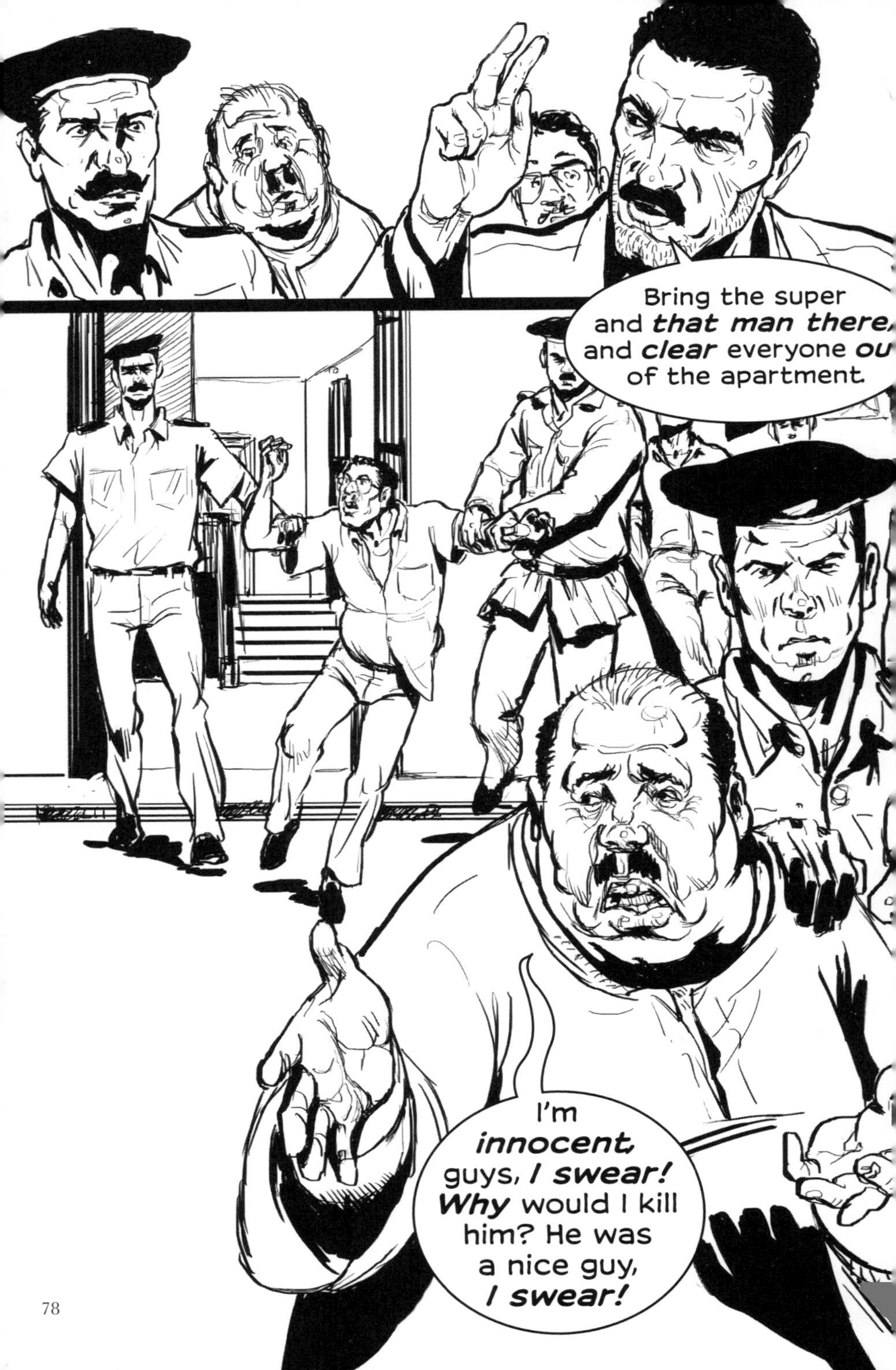
Bring the super and *that man there,* and *clear* everyone *ou* of the apartment.
I'm *innocent,* guys, *I swear! Why* would I kill him? He was a nice guy, *I swear!*

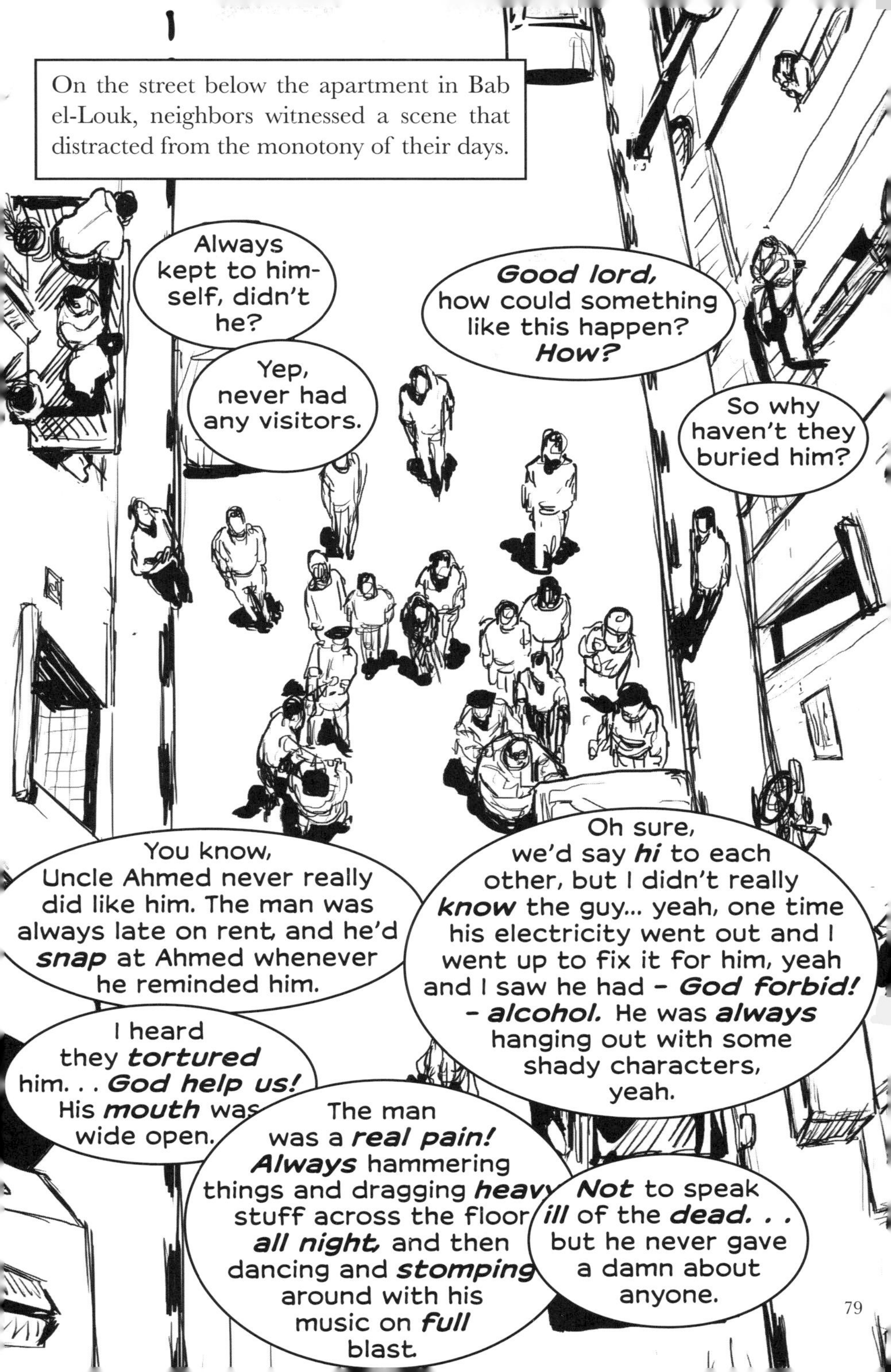
On the street below the apartment in Bab el-Louk, neighbors witnessed a scene that distracted from the monotony of their days.
Always kept to him-self, didn't he?
Yep, never had any visitors.
Good lord, how could something like this happen? How?
So why haven't they buried him?
You know, Uncle Ahmed never really did like him. The man was always late on rent, and he'd snap at Ahmed whenever he reminded him.
Oh sure, we'd say hi to each other, but I didn't really know the guy... yeah, one time his electricity went out and I went up to fix it for him, yeah and I saw he had – God forbid! – alcohol. He was always hanging out with some shady characters, yeah.
I heard they tortured him. . . God help us! His mouth was wide open.
The man was a real pain! Always hammering things and dragging heavy stuff across the floor all night, and then dancing and stomping around with his music on full blast.
Not to speak ill of the dead. . . but he never gave a damn about anyone.

The end.

To my neighbors in
Bab el-Louk

The man who keeps pigeons, and
his pigeon loft, the two hawks who
fought on the roof across from me,
the sad-looking house, the showers,
the protests I saw from my window,
the coffeehouses filled with drunks,
suspicious encounters in the square
at four in the morning, people and
their children awake at all hours,
ambling along the sidewalk in front
of the market, the annoying woman
next door, the fat woman next door
who spends the whole day washing
clothes and hanging them out to
dry, her fat lonely son, the doctor's
patients waiting on the balcony, all
the doctors' signs, Chamber of In-
dustry and parliamentary election
season signs, the sound of the shut-
ters moving in the wind, and the
Nubian family next door.

- Donia Maher

Donia Maher is an Egyptian author with a background in Scenography and Marketing. She has worked as an actress, director, and designer of sets and costumes.

Ganzeer is an artist whose output includes installations, prints, paintings, videos, objects, comix, and guerrilla actions in public space.

Ahmad Nady graduated wih honors from the Oil Painting Department of the Faculty of Fine Arts in Cairo, 2003. His professional career started in 1999 on the first season of "Alam Semsem" (Arabic Sesame Street). He has since created editorial cartoons, comics, animation, and TV commercials. He is the recepient of a number of awards from festivals and art-focused websites.

Elisabeth Jaquette is a translator from the Arabic, whose work has appeared in The New York Times, the Guardian, and elsewhere. She is the recipient of a PEN/Heim Translation Award and an English PEN Translates Award, and was a CASA Fellow at the American University in Cairo. Elisabeth is also managing director of the American Literary Translators Association.